THE EIGHTH DAY

THE EIGHTH DAY

KEYS TO AN OPEN DOOR

SELECTED WRITINGS OF CHRISTIAN BOBIN

Translated by Pauline Matarasso

DARTON · LONGMAN + TODD

First published in 2015 by
Darton, Longman and Todd Ltd
1 Spencer Court
140–142 Wandsworth High Street
London SW18 4JJ

ISBN 978-0-232-53171-8

A catalogue record for this book is available from the British Library.

Phototypeset by Kerrypress Ltd

Printed and bound by ScandBook AB

To the Benedictine Community at
Howton Grove Priory

Contents

Acknowledgements

My thanks go first to the begetter of this book, Christian Bobin, who from the outset has been wholly generous, insisting that his books belonged to their readers and inviting me to make myself at home and wander round at whim. The translator, he said, ended up knowing every nook and cranny.

My son, François, has played more than one part. A challenge thrown out to me to translate a sentence from a Bobin book picked up by chance, led, four years later, to his fielding urgent emails saying: Which of these versions is better? He was (almost) always right.

Much gratitude goes to Paul Keegan for his preface, written with a discernment that Christian Bobin would appreciate. His close reading of Bobin's work and the wide frame of reference in which he sets it will help to open up the texts to new readers.

My thanks go out also to Ann Wroe, Martin Laird, Martha Reeves and Andrew Louth, who have offered generous support in different and valued ways, and lastly but by no means least, to DLT in the person of David Moloney, for trusting his judgment and offering English readers a book which will be a pleasure to look at, read and handle.

Copyright Acknowledgements

'The Eighth Day of the Week': translated with permission from *Le Huitième jour de la semaine* © Les Éditions Lettres Vives, 1986.

'Queen, King, Jack': translated with permission from *Dame, roi, valet* © Éditions Gallimard, 1994.

'Look at Me, Look at Me' and 'Get Moving, Jonah, I'm Waiting': translated with permission from *Une petite robe de fête* © Éditions Gallimard, 1991. North American rights granted by permission © Autumn Hill Press, 2009.

'A World of Distance': translated with permission from *L'Éloignement du monde* © Les Éditions Lettres Vives, 1993.

'Mozart and the Rain': translated with permission from *Mozart et la pluie* © Les Éditions Lettres Vives, 1997.

'The Tightrope Walker': translated with permission from *L'Equilibriste* © Le temps qu'il fait, 1998.

'Pure Presence': translated with permission from *La Présence pure* © Le temps qu'il fait, 2002.

'Resurrection': translated with permission from *Ressusciter* © Éditions Gallimard, 2001.

Acknowledgements

'A Killer White as Snow': translated with permission from *Un Assassin blanc comme neige* © Éditions Gallimard, 2011.

'The Joy-Man': translated with permission from *L'Homme joie* © Christian Bobin et l'Iconoclaste, Paris, 2012.

Preface

by Paul Keegan

*We should instead be wandering through our
lives as though we were no longer there, with
the litheness of a cat in the long grass.*

'There are very few events in a life,' suggests Christian
Bobin, and for many of us only a single unfolding event:
that of our slow submersion in the common round, in
a world that demands our unwavering attention. And
succeeds, because society itself has become the major
superstition of our times, with its claim to be the crucible
of all human meanings.

Bobin's surprising but perfectly chosen image for our
modern bondage is drawn from the early eighteenth-
century *Mémoires* of the duc de Saint-Simon, the
unsleeping Boswell of the French court: 'They assemble
at Versailles, crowding round Louis XIV, the picture-
book king, and this is their sole employment: being
present. They contemplate each other in the uncertain
light of candles…'

By this act of compliance – 'being present' – we face
away from what matters, now as then. Or rather, we
focus on the essentials and neglect the rest, 'forgetting
that the essential is none other than what we neglect'.
We lose our bearings, we face away from the day and its
sufficiency, we forget that we have no home other than

in the ordinary, with its lack of directives or direction, its tracklessness.

But this is already too garrulous. Christian Bobin's writings, their formulas and questions, are invariably limpid and exact: 'So what is ordinary life, where we are and yet are not?' The answer is that it is something sheer and formidable, which is why we try hard not to linger there. Above all it is solitary: a place whose borders are defended by boredom; whose speech is 'a language without desire', whose time is a stopped clock, where the self waits without waiting, like 'a hive emptied of its bees'.

Bobin embraces this fallow state: 'I love these hours as one can love an awkward child … Yes, I love this barren, inglorious time. It saves me from being someone.' This is an unfamiliar thought, like news from a foreign country, even if others than Bobin have been there before. The psychoanalyst D. W. Winnicott wrote that we are at our most idiosyncratic when most anonymously alone, as if personality were invented for the purpose of compliance. Or in the words of Emily Dickinson (to whom Bobin recently devoted a brief 'imaginary' biography): 'I'm nobody! Who are you? / Are you nobody, too?' – followed by a whisper of conspiracy: 'How dreary to be somebody!'

So who is this nobody, Christian Bobin, who bears the same allegorical name as Bunyan's pilgrim? It is easier to say what he has been than who he is, and Pauline Matarasso's introduction gives us essential signposts: by turns a philosophy student, a civil servant, a psychiatric nurse, a solitary thinker who has spent a lifetime (he was born in 1951) in or near Le Creusot, a corner of rural Burgundy where his forbears lived and worked, his father as draughtsman for the Schneider iron mills. As for Bobin's belief, it is Christian, but pared down, like a primitive church, taking the shape and form – as he remarks – of the faces he meets in his daily life.

At all points in time he has been a writer, though he sees himself as undefined rather than defined by writing, which for him is a means and not an end. His works remain largely untranslated in English, yet are published by the mainstream and august house of Gallimard in Paris. Widespread recognition came with a short peripatetic life of St Francis of Assisi, written in 1992. In the following decades his books have sold in quietly astonishing numbers – yet their audience (or readership, rather, with all this implies of an individual encounter) is elusive, hard to define, perhaps as hidden or 'anonymous' as the author himself.

As Pauline Matarasso says, in her luminously translated selection of short texts, Bobin 'has published novels, stories, essays, biographical works, none of which exactly fits the genre to which it apparently belongs'. His themes are simple: nature, childhood, parents, momentary encounters, aloneness, the eventlessness of the everyday as it strikes a receptive apparatus of exceptional resilience and inwardness – and, yes, idiosyncrasy. He has no theories, no expertise, no claim to vision. He looks and listens, and for him writing reciprocates seeing.

Visible and invisible, two words for the same thing. William Blake is one of Bobin's tutelary spirits, and he would approve Blake's question (asked by a devil in

Hell): 'How do you know but ev'ry Bird that cuts the airy way is an immense world of delight, clos'd by your senses five?' But Bobin is not a mystic – no more than Blake – nor a pantheist, if such labels suggest a frictionless or privileged access to transcendent truths. His world is too wry, too this-worldly, too touched by humour and oddity, too peopled. Instead, we may find echoes or traces of Bobin's sensibility at unexpected turns: from the Stoic doctrine that you must find your place (and then know it) to the humanism of Gaston Bachelard, with its phenomenology of minute particulars. Or we find him again (and again) in the essays of Montaigne, who also thought long and hard about fallowness, about the border and barter between world and self, the differences between wisdom and furious enterprise.

A fellow melancholic, Montaigne advised setting aside an *arrière-boutique* – a room for ourselves at the back of the shop, as a place of retreat, where no business is allowed, and instead of *negotium* there is *otium* (learnèd leisure, in Montaigne's case). In its plainness, this back-room sounds véry like Bobin, who also philosophises in a makeshift place, along the stopping points of 'a life whose every instant is without a template'.

Bobin's vagrant ethos – his hedgerow indigence – defines both him and his belief ('The singular grace of a neglected garden makes a strong case for a gypsy God.') But here a delicate transaction is involved. Bobin prizes resistance, above all, and the need to defend our solitude in relation to our time in this life. But in relation to all that is not us – to all that is eternity's portion, so to speak – 'we need to relax our grip and accept what comes, holding on to nothing. Rejecting all on the one hand, accepting all on the other'. What is desired is for the world to recede – and know its place – in order that something else, solitary and silent, may approach.

For Bobin, who is uninterested in the luxury of introspection, we receive what is inside us from *without* – and everything hides in the open. Sometimes he sounds like a Christian cousin of Kafka, the Kafka who could write: 'You do not need to leave your room. Remain sitting at your table and listen. Do not even listen, simply wait, be quite still and solitary. The world will freely offer itself to you to be unmasked, it has no choice, it will roll in ecstasy at your feet.' And he has something of Kafka's cunning, his undeceived anticipation of the self and its traps: 'We need to guard, not only against the world, but against our preoccupation with ourselves, another door by which the world might creep back in like a prowler into a sleeping house.' As Montaigne said, we must get away from the crowd out there, but also from the crowd inside ourselves. We are the obstacle that stands between us and an unobstructed view.

What I most admire in Bobin, almost, is his unexpected ferocity. His distrust of public faces in private places: 'A lofty self-awareness goes hand in hand with an inwardly depressive state – as an empire that has lost its self-belief fortifies its frontiers and takes a pride in its tombs.' His flat rejection of experience as involving ownership – rather than tenancy – of what is experienced. Or the way he looks out on the world, reads the papers and tracks the enemy: the tentacular and self-replicating siren whose blinking computer screens tell us not to look with our own eyes; persuading us that it will spend our time for us, that it knows what we do not know. Bobin sniffs for signs and waits for the regime to falter and crash.

He is beautifully acerbic, for example, about places, and how the very idea of place is diminished by the anxious inanities of a society that converts everything into spectacle. 'From a distance, Strasbourg station, encased in its convex glass surround, looks like a liqueur-filled sweet. Close up it is harrowing, like railway stations everywhere'. 'The small towns that tourism catches in its resin of perfection … stones that over-admiration has rendered soulless.' Even churches are not safe from the disarmament of his gaze: 'Maguelone cathedral, built of stones hauled up from the adjacent sea, is a great empty shell: God the Hermit Crab has left.'

Solitude is a way of seeing rather than a pious removal. And what it sees is far from bad news: namely that the infra-ordinary and eventless are replete with animate life, with the gods in things, or with the exemplary because pointless doings of the very old and the very young. Moreover, Bobin is philosophically reconciled on the subject of communication and its chimeras: 'The spoken word is never heard exactly as it's said: once we have accepted that, we can move around at ease in speech, wholly unconcerned with being understood, careful only to keep our speech as close as possible to our lives.' Consequently he has time to pay attention to what he hears rather than what he says.

One section of this book is set in a care home for elderly Alzheimer's patients, who include Bobin's father. Like the other texts it is perfectly cantilevered, or dramatised (Bobin is a writer, not a purveyor of aphorisms), alternating between what occurs in 'this house of last resort' and the daily doings of a tree outside the window, until at last he has them in alignment. He notices everything, even-handedly, including 'the little man whose Parkinson's shakes him like a tinkling bell'. Another section is set in the retirement home of his mother, where even the absent are present to him:

> The man in the room next to my mother's died two weeks after his arrival in the home. Enough time for me to see something of his elegance, his weariness and his soul, worn as thin as a used bar of soap that keeps slipping through the fingers. His name has disappeared from the door of his room, and the gleam of the newly white card sears like a mystery.

> My mother, another resident, my sister and I sit facing the roses under the midnight-green rain of the cherry tree, with a bottle of champagne placed on the gravel like the mad knight in a giant chess set. Gaiety takes possession of drinkers *before* they drink.

> In a room on the first floor [of the retirement home] a van Gogh poster – sunflowers in a brass pot – wrestles in vain with a woman in an armchair, her head lolling on her chest like an unstrung puppet's: the sunflowers' potency bows before the little broken soul.

Engagement rather than withdrawal is increasingly the thing to wonder at as we progress through this book – attachment tempered by the steel of solitude, as of like calling to like: 'A very old lady enters the cutler's shop in Beaune. She has a head like a vine peach stone and eyes of grey fire. She is funny, distinguished, up for the adventure of a real conversation. She admits to being so lonely that she hears "the noise of the light bulb" when eating in her kitchen.'

Looking at the surfaces of everything, Bobin treats everything – animate and inanimate – within the same optic, devoid of 'irritable searching' after facts, not least the supposed facts of the self. As Pauline Matarasso says: 'Trees are important to Bobin as paradigms of acceptance, which is not the same as resignation.' There is something pre-Socratic about Bobin's world of wind and tree and stones and stars: 'The wind visits every leaf of the plane tree without omitting one.' But there is something as close to us as our own breath in his apprehension of the creaturely: 'The eyes of the dormouse shine like a night at the opera'; 'a startled lizard jumps down a drain – another one that mustn't be forgotten.'

All roads run past God, but God in these pages often runs for his life, and takes many forms (at one point glimpsed as a boar with bristles bolting across the road, crashing into the undergrowth). Bobin's God can be teased, or teased out. Their relationship has a combative, Jonah-like aspect.

Indeed the wisdom of this book is far from unitary or passive; on the contrary it is plural and partisan: 'Each of us is born with a solitary task to fulfil and those we meet on our way help or hinder us in its completion: alas for the one who is unable to distinguish between them.' His writing persuades us that here we have one manifold definition of being alive – as a position without defences. 'All we can do is welcome it … It borrows our body for a while and will outlive it.' Again, we think of the ancient Greeks – and I think again of Winnicott, the practitioner of a modern and wholly secular practice of the self – which may seem a farfetched connection, but whose originality was comparably hard-won and patient, who wrote that 'it is a constant struggle to get to the starting point, and to stay there.'

Introduction

by Pauline Matarasso

A few years ago, when I first came across the writings of Christian Bobin, I did not expect to be presenting him to English-speaking readers. With a reputation in France long established and a succession of slim volumes welcomed by a large following, one might have expected him to have made an earlier passage across the Channel. Although two of his books have appeared in the US, he remains virtually unknown here, in part because his output is not easily classifiable. This selection, drawn from a number of works published between 1985 and 2012, has been prepared as a tempter. Christian Bobin is a fine enough writer to need no further explanation, and readers may wish to plunge straight in, but those who prefer a context to accompany the encounter will find some brief reflections on the relationship between his life and writing below. They are of doubtful value, since, on his own authority, 'the man people talk about when they discuss [his] books does not exist'.

Born in 1951 – one of the few life events he has been unable to avoid – in Le Creusot, a Burgundian town with a long industrial and mining history, Christian Bobin has always lived within a metaphorical stone's throw of his birthplace. Now rooted, hermit-like, in a small patch of countryside, his gaze, again like that of hermits, rests either on the minute particularity of his surroundings or on what is beyond vision. Having read his way through childhood, he studied philosophy at the university of Dijon and spent some years working unenthusiastically as a civil servant. A stint as a student psychiatric nurse may have confirmed, as well as complementing, his views on the human condition derived from introspection and from books. Writing was initially a way of learning to live with himself and of introducing, into what he perceived as the universal shipwreck, a degree less of order than of elegance. Short texts were being published regularly from 1984 onwards by small presses and finding favour with both reviewers and a growing public. As soon as his earnings covered his very moderate needs Bobin gave up his job. To say that he now writes full time is true in the sense that he does nothing else, but doing nothing is for him an essential, if not a full time, occupation.

That sixty years of life can be summed up in a paragraph speaks – and has spoken – volumes. Dates, events, any sense of a willed, let alone planned, progression through the years are as absent as Bobin has been able to make them, partly because he sets no value by these things, and partly because, setting no value by them, he has ensured there would be as few as he could manage. 'I don't remember ever wanting this or that kind of life. From childhood on I have put my every effort into refusing whatever was proposed to me, pushed by something I couldn't put a name to and still can't.' This refusal of an 'eventful life', further hedged around by privacy, sits paradoxically with the reality that much of his work is a process of self-revelation. He inhabits his texts, thinking aloud, telling a story, going for a walk, cutting his finger doing the washing up. His uneventful days are the context in and through which he explores the existential questions about life, death and meaning. The determination with which he pursues the indefinable, as well as the skill he employs to pin it down, can only be exercised, he would claim, in silence and reclusion.

As a writer Bobin is no less adept at eluding categorisation. He has published novels, stories, essays, biographical works, none of which exactly fits the genre to which it apparently belongs. What he does most frequently and best is to address the great existential questions through a reversed telescope, drawing in the parameters of his own life to intensify his view. In this he takes his place in the tradition of Montaigne, while working on a much smaller canvas and with a more spiritual focus. He holds out one hand to Montaigne and extends the other, reverentially, towards Pascal. But unlike these great predecessors, Bobin is a poet – not a title he claims for himself, but one given him by critics, peers and readers. This is not necessarily obvious to anyone opening one of his books who is unfamiliar with the concept of prose poetry. The prose poem evolved in France, where it became an accepted genre in the nineteenth century – favoured by Baudelaire among others – and found distinguished practitioners among the Symbolists and their successors. Adopted with enthusiasm by German poets, the form spread across Europe before being taken up by the Beat Generation in the United States. The freedom it allows opened up fresh paths for poets practised in traditional forms, Rimbaud, Rilke and

Mallarmé among them. The prose poem is normally a short work of a page or two, and might be described as a poem in undress. But however casual it may outwardly appear, the thought that inhabits it is that of a poet. In the words of a French literary critic: 'whatever a poet may think, he thinks it as a poet;' to this one might add, even when he appears to be writing in prose.

Bobin does not set out to write prose poems. He writes about life as he sees it. He just happens to see it as a poet. To say that he is interpreting the world through his feelings, his emotions, if partly true, is to oversimplify: he is *seeing* it in a different way, and both his life and writing, each consonant with the other, reflect his manner of seeing. In this he is not unlike Blake, to whom he nods in admiration. His thought processes are lateral, sometimes circular, often sudden. He is at home with metaphor, at ease, like Rilke, with a religious vocabulary ('soul', 'eternity', 'angel') freed from the constraint of doctrinal precision.

He is a patient observer of the natural world, but not a dispassionate one. He engages with it like a lover, one drawn to the small, the plain and easily overlooked, to daisies, sparrows, pebbles, water skaters on a pond. He is a contemplative and it is as such that he writes about nature, trying to pin on the page the strength and also the fragility of what he has met with on his walk, always afraid of crushing it with words. For him the natural world is primarily the purveyor of wonder, but also has lessons for us in patience, in humility, in giving without return.

He is the poet too of all that is wounded or vulnerable, in particular of the very old and the very young, writing with rare tenderness and insight about dementia and childhood. And if the old are generally his father, the child is always in some way himself. His books are peopled with children – Hélène, aged five when he first met her, and, ten years later, her four-year-old sister Clémence, as well as a nameless procession who rightly sense in him another fugitive from the grown-up world. Himself the youngest in an outwardly ordinary family, yet aware at an early age of being a misfit, Bobin has retained a child's eye view of life. It is not his only perspective – far from it – but it is uniquely his, which is why his readers so often find themselves looking at the familiar in an unexpected light. Childhood is seen as intrinsically good. It is the reverse of all he detests in the 'serious' world of jobs, commerce and conflict. Unless we become as little children there is no hope for us. He, happily, has not lost that state, which he now gleans for metaphors. His life is 'like a boisterous child'. At times of inner dereliction he is 'sequestered like a child sent supperless to bed'. But happily – for some fasts are necessary – no one comes to revoke the punishment, and when the child emerges in the morning, he washes the darkness from his face in rainwater and finds life waiting for him out of doors.

Bobin is above all the poet of joy – joy and wonder – 'joy that overtops the greatest pain and yet does not abate it'. Like all joy, it has been hard won. A lifelong sufferer from 'persuasive melancholy', he has spent most of it mining the narrow seam of joy in the dank rock face of depression, and writing has been the tool he has employed to chip it out. Writing has been for him lifesaving, but it has also over the years become a form of gift, ultimately a self-offering: what he has crafted he hands over, lets go, and passes on. 'I only like books with pages soaked in blue – the blue that has stood the test of death. If my sentences smile, it is because they come out of the dark ... My smile costs me a fortune.' For this he has made himself a master craftsman. He works with a limited vocabulary and uses it with the precision of a watchmaker, often obtaining his effects through startling juxtapositions of the ordinary, aiming straight at the heart and not without the intention of drawing blood. To this end he has evolved an extraordinarily pared-down style, a distillation. The poetry is not in the words, but in the seeing, his, and also in the hearing, ours. Poets were seers, singers and tellers long before they were writers. Bobin invites us to read his words as a score and hear them in all their musicality, his sentences supplying the rhythm, balance and cadences that echo the wide range of music-makers he admires.

An anthology offers the advantage of a bird's-eye view of an evolving life and talent. An author can be observed passing from youth to age between two covers. With a writer like Bobin, who uses his own life as a magnifier to focus and direct attention on the greater questions, a pattern can be seen emerging from the clues enigmatically scattered through the text. It so happens that a key piece to the puzzle that is Bobin's life is missing here. It is found in the book-length elegy published in 1999, and entitled *La Plus que vive*, commemorating the life and sudden death of the woman he loved, an event so shocking, so intensely felt that he could not keep it out of his work. It was a relationship in which the parameters were set by the woman, fought against briefly by the man and finally found to deepen and define it. She may properly be termed his muse, in that his works from 'The Eighth Day of the Week' until her death ten years later, and probably beyond, were written under her metaphorical eye and within the life-giving warmth of her love. In that early and important work she already has a coded presence and her daughter Hélène a real one. In 'The Tightrope Walker' she is the beloved of Bobin the circus performer telling his story to Bobin the sacked insurance clerk. A vignette in 'The Killer White as Snow' represents her close to death in hospital, while Bobin cares for the four-year-old Clémence. *La Plus que vive* is a deeply moving fusion of distance and intimacy, where once again the minutiae of life interpret and reflect the universal. Reducing it to excerpts would do it a grave injustice, but to know it exists gives an added density to passages in other works.

Presenting thirty years of a writer's work (even in translation) is an endorsement of its artistic value, and, as such, it raises questions both of value and reception. Who determines the worth of these texts: the critics who sit in judgement, the publishers and booksellers who market the product, or the readers who buy it? In the 1980s the emerging Bobin was classed as a 'difficult' writer and his ultra-slim volumes interleaved with space were shelved as 'literature' or 'poetry'. As his readership grew and widened, and the big publishers moved in, there was a clear critical shift: he couldn't after all be difficult and his writing should be downgraded to 'spirituality'.

Bobin himself gives his word to the beloved that he will never write for effect ('écrire de la littérature' are the words she uses with distaste). Three days after this exchange, she had died and it became a promise sealed. But both surely would be just as horrified at the idea of writing 'spirituality', or indeed anything at all that could have a name put to it. He writes; that's all. If his work had not evolved over time it would not be worth anthologising. It has become less obviously difficult, but paradoxically the pursuit of the simple has rendered it more complex and profound. The poet would like more white on the page (or sometimes blue), to reflect the growing space in his head. He has learnt to say more with less. Religion is more readily acknowledged as interlocutor: some conflicts are on the way to resolution. One reader's evocative online response to Bobin's latest book, *La Grande Vie*: 'Having given it some thought, I realise that this writer makes me happy', unconsciously echoes Bobin himself in *Le Christ aux coquelicots*: 'When they asked me how I understood your word, I heard myself say: "I am happy."' Giving it still further thought, the same reader finds that the happiness evoked by reading Bobin is identical to the feelings woken in him by certain painters.

Professional judgements of literary (or spiritual) value are neither as disinterested nor as definite as they sometimes seem. They are, in the end, only the responses of readers to texts. Christian Bobin writes: we read. It is enough to do it with an open heart. The rest will take care of itself: it always does.

xxx

THE EIGHTH DAY OF THE WEEK

This is the most important of Bobin's early texts, in which his principal themes are already present and explored in depth: childhood, nature, death, time and timelessness, the role of writing in the life of the writer, and that of the writer as translator and interpreter of what he sees. The eighth day is the day that follows the Jewish Sabbath when God rested from creating. It is thus beyond time. It is also the first day of the Christian week, the day that saw all made new.

The work, divided into six sections, opens with the words: 'My life is like a boisterous child', and Bobin, along with other children, some named, some not, flits in and out of these pages, alternating with reflections on childhood as a state, the child as symbol of escape and rebellion, as well as the new-born, seen as retaining a pre-birth knowledge of the eternal. This state is far from idyllic – the writer returns frequently to the suffering of childhood: 'the knowledge that all fails absolutely will take the child a long time to dilute in the bloodstream, burn in autumnal reading or disperse in the stress of a job'.

The child is also that in us which refuses to connive with the straitjacketed adult world. The alternative – to give one's whole attention to the present, living with open hands, which allows us to slip out of time and into the eighth day of the week – is every bit as hard: 'What we take at times for detachment is merely indifference or resignation – just two more metamorphoses of the ego.' In the face of death, which haunts this text as it does most of Bobin's work, 'there is no escape route, since there is no route'. It is only in silence and the mute attention to the immediate that we will find our place in the absolute that surrounds us.

In section 4, one of his most lyrical pieces, Bobin takes a walk with the lover, *l'amoureuse*, who remains wonderfully undefined: woman, nature, muse, god – spring is as close as he gets – and, like all of these, she is unbiddable. Silence alone can be depended on. And it is silence that leads once more into the theme of death and back again into childhood: 'As though the two silences – that of death swaddled in life and that of life winkled from death – had not always been one and the same, the silence of childhood in its boundless grief, in its eternal laughter.' Finally 'The Eighth Day of the Week' ends with a child's question, a question that only a child can ask directly, without irony or political agenda: 'What is beauty?' Again man and child go for a walk, looking and talking late into the gloaming. 'In the silence we'd discover at last, he and I, the answer to his question. In the luminous vastness of a silence that words caress without disturbing it.'

A brief note on the words sung by the angelic voice in section II. They represent the refrain from a traditional song, 'À la claire fontaine', familiar to all French children: 'Il y a longtemps que je t'aime, Jamais je ne t'oublierai'. Rendering songs is the translator's nightmare. It needs to be done to the silent accompaniment of the tune, which determines where the accents fall and which syllables are sustained and require open vowels. This is a song bathed in nostalgia for a lost love and the air has the dying fall so prized ('that strain again!') by Orsino. The words 't'oublierai' consist of three open vowels which can be sustained at will. The words 'forget you' are all but unsingable: those offered are an attempt to translate to the silence of the page two elements that need sound to make sense.

'Would that the rose were still on the tree' is from the same song; 'And if the cricket sleeps there, do it no wrong' is a line from the still older 'Nous n'irons plus aux bois'.

THE EIGHTH DAY OF THE WEEK

I

My life is like a boisterous child that has just come home, excited from an outdoor game: it is always leaving me, returning at intervals in a wrought-up state that a few words are enough to calm. I write very little, and that little is still too much, in relation to the scattered instants which light the path I travel by: there are very few events in a life. Sometimes the only event is that of its disaster, its slow engulfing in the disaster of the common round, which sees our energies drain away into the polluted mishmash of our days. So what is ordinary life, where we are and yet are not? It is a language without desire, a time devoid of wonder. Sickly-sweet as a lie. I know that state by heart – that is where I experience its banality and violence. The soul, in that state, is like a hive emptied of its bees. The soul (which is to say the body, the dawn, every name in the world, for all names are petals of a unique dream flower) – the soul disengages, slips off, grows bored. Wilts. Two or three weeks go by like this, four at the most: an eternity, the one that governs sleep and stones. During all this time I can't write, not even letters: I am devoid of truth. What is the use of telling stories if I myself have turned into a dull and graceless fiction? I have always known these interludes of absence and I always shall. They don't bother me. Not any longer. I love these hours as one can love an awkward child, one who has no wish to please, with a love neither justifiable nor justified. By ignoring our wishes, by evading all demands, this child enriches us without our knowing. He forces us to foster in ourselves the selfless love that will allow us to hug him without holding: a love that knows no limit because its end eludes it, an attention rendered boundless by incessant disappointments. Yes, I love this barren, inglorious time. It saves me from being someone, it sets me aside, sequestered like a child sent supperless to bed. It is like a time of fasting or betrothal. Like keeping a wake for one who is absent and preserving undisturbed the dust on his name. Unable to write, and living out a penitential time that sheds its hours as a tree sheds leaves, I read. I devour books, and not a word brings succour. It's a common enough experience: this gulf between weighty knowledge, as embalmed in books or moral laws, and the breezy mood of life as it passes. One can be a mine of learning and spend one's life in total ignorance of life. It is not the books that are to blame, but the meagreness of our desire, the narrow limits of our dreaming. At bottom, if truth is sometimes lacking in us, it's because we first failed truth, by claiming to direct and know her. So it is right for her to punish us and send us back into the dark, dismissed with a reprimand recalling us to our solitude, as to some long-neglected homework. Time passes, these empty hours that I am unwrapping here while talking about them. No one comes to fetch the punished child, the daydreamer. Happily, no one revokes the punishment, and he is left, uninterrupted, to a stupendous view of eternity, of night and of the soul. In the morning, when he emerges, he washes the darkness from his face in a little rainwater. Life returns, as a slight pulse felt in the temples. Beauty is there, out of doors: on the underside of chestnuts on the paths, in the angle of a window, on the dark fruit of brambles and the dust of the roads, in the green of rivers – everywhere. Beauty, which is to say life. Life, massive and tenuous, life without lesions. Life with no make-up on. It is amid this luxuriance of the unknown that I am turning this evening the pages of an art book, contemplating paintings. With their placing of a cloud in the sky, or an orange on a plate, painters bring out what evening still contains of day, invent the exact distance that allows space to open up and love to dance. Painting's lesson is about goodness: we recognise love in this attention to detail, the care for minutiae, the respect for what we are entrusted with and that a snatch would annihilate, like a sparrow squeezed in a grasping hand. The humblest things – fruits and stones, grasses and stars alike – invite us to an endless feast-day, and to enjoy it we have to learn the immediacy of mental touch which is the privilege of painters. That endless practice of gentleness, that willing of simplicity. In the evening of his life Matisse paints with scissors. He cuts straight out of the sky thunderclouds of pure wine and springtimes of blue silk. He rediscovers the simple magic of coloured crayons. Day after day he plucks the calm hours, as a child counts its joys one by one before falling asleep. He is old, he is ill. It is in the years of suffering that he greets a star, and under the arcades of old age that he dresses childhood in flowers. Night is coming to meet him. She has the sweetness of a girl and the freshness of a wellspring. He paints. He paints as one smiles or as one dies. He walks along a path that is impassable and radiant. He steals two chords of a song to celebrate the joy that overtops the greatest pain and yet does not abate it: long live rose and lilac yet. The painter is going away. Heading deep into a garden open to the seasons and to apple scrumpers, with shards of light falling through his fingers. But Matisse's name is of little importance: the names of beauty are nobody's names. The names of beauty are the names of a nerve tendril, an abyss in the blood, a condition of the world; and the paper blown along the street by the wind, the transparency of a fruit or the mould on an old staircase teach us as much about beauty and the soul as the lightnings summoned into the sky by great painters. These, when their art is at its simplest, do no more than espouse the common beauty, serve her and praise her. If they give her their name, it is like giving one's name to the king's daughter in the vain hope that she might not forget you utterly on her wedding night. It's the same as throwing, on the hurt of living, an abundance of roses and lilac.

II

From our earliest days we know all that needs to be known: eternity is a smell, a voice that sings and softens till words are lost. Death is the same thing, a fragrance, the sound of a door slamming, a glass breaking. The new-born child is dependent on what draws near, on what moves away, is dependent on everything, since everything comes, happens – be it fly, angel, or fright. But before all these things, and first to come, there is the mother, mistress of speech and therefore of silence. Her voice is the voice of rivers, always even, always musical, night and day alike. The water of language streams over the new-born's flesh. The dust of long-dead stars brushes its cheeks. A silence strokes its fingernails. Shawled in a forename, it falls asleep among the angels and their counsellors. Its body bathes in the boundlessness of a presence free of harm. Its soul – closed and tender – is wrapped in the poor cloth of a song: *Long, long have I loved you: never will I turn away.* This voice from the dawning has never left my ears, even if the enchanted words grew shadowy with time. It guided secretly my ways of loving and losing. Listening to this song that was given me with the day, and waiting for what would never come – since it had always been – I kept as close as possible to the sleeping child. At times the voice grew very faint. In the world it was stifled, and perhaps the world is nothing more than that: the wrong kind of silence imposed on our lives. On one such night among many, I found the voice again in that heavy book which clutters up my days: Saint-Simon's *Memoirs*. Its language is grating, full of splinters and brilliant lightning flashes. Poisoned with saccharine. The book is wadded in its ink and buckled in its gall. The narrator never steps aside. Everything is noted, skewered with a pin. The narrator never sleeps. He speaks of his own kind; he speaks of the appalling void his kind generate, without, within, and all around them. He is speaking of the nobles, those who never move, eat or die save ensconced in their possessions and surrounded by their peers. They assemble at Versailles, crowding round Louis XIV, the picture-book king, and it's their sole employment: being present. Persisting in this nullity of luxury and mirrors. They contemplate each other in the uncertain light of candles. The court provides these insatiable spectators with a round-the-clock performance. Death agonies, long-drawn, are presented as entertainments. The chamber of suffering is open like the others and audience is held there. Many die each year, yet the mass of nobles stays entire – the horde of princes, counts and duchesses, the ermine collars and lace sleeves with the grime beneath. They come, they go: a tiny world in fact, and, as never before, the one and only. There is the odd rain shower. One who withdraws – and it's his salvation – one who leaves the circle and retires to his property, entering the chill of a cloister or of a train of thought. But the sum stays the same, the gross mass of people, opinions and forces. It's an age away from us, the world of the early eighteenth century, and yet it is substantially our own. Its brilliance easily surpasses that of dream or love. Its brilliance is without compare. Evil has its purity, darkness its light. What is lacking in this book, what is missing from the world? Little by little one grows aware: children, animals, trees and rivers are all missing. There is nothing but adults on their own, nothing but grey souls. The poor, too, are missing. People languish from boredom, never from hunger. And the words of the poor are missing; missing, the snatch of a popular song, and missing, the voice shot through with stars from the world that has been dismissed. Guardian of the light-filled hours, it will have been heard on the thresholds of death and birth, and, between the sheen of the new-born and the pallor of the dying, nothing will have happened: a silence between two notes of light. An interval between two seasons. The blink of an eye. The time required by the angel, bent over the drowsy child, to take a breath and sing the phrase right through: *Long, long have I loved you: never will I turn away.*

III

Walking the narrow footpath of a memory, one comes now and then across a strayed light, snagged in the green burn of brambles. Its wing is broken. It has lost its sisters. Everything that happens to us outlives us in this way – as a suffering in space. Suspended. Floating free of both words and the absence of words. No book can save us from our life. No words are able to cushion those shards that return to prick us, and so prevent the descent of evening, the coming of peace. We exist in time, bowed down by death. There is no escape route, since there is no route. There is no consolation, since everything wounds, but nothing kills us. There is just what lies in front of our eyes and the light that falls on it. Just these water skaters that I watch skimming the silk of a pond, flimsy, proceeding by fits and starts, as though actuated by a thought process repeatedly broken off and taken up again, inventing the lightness of a way between the two massive eternities of air and water. It is with words as tenuous as their legs that I write, their instinct that I borrow to let my hand slide over the grain of the page, between ink and air. I lack their grace. I lack the delicacy of their lineaments and the simplicity of their hours. I watch them at length – the time it takes for me to move inwardly to the brink of the unknown, that highest form of knowledge: dream, and the worship of silence. One never surrenders in vain to that elemental beauty which ravishes the soul into the spiral of a star, an insect, or any created thing: this certitude brings calm to the hours when I don't write and to those when I do. It lights up the night and its angelic sister, solitude. Silence is the highest form of thought, and it is in developing in us this mute attention to the day, that we will find our place in the absolute that surrounds us. It falls to us – when all things fail us and depart – to give to our life the patience of a work of art, the flexibility of reeds under the rough hand of the wind, a homage paid to winter. A little silence is enough. A little of that intangible food of silence which one's mother dispensed when reading a story that hollowed out the night and set its depths ablaze: *Once upon a time there was a woodcutter and his wife who had seven children, all boys; the eldest was only ten years old and the youngest no more than seven.* The words echoed in the crystal space of sleep. The story flowed through lengths of time, its waters decking themselves with straws of light as they carried away the ogre's knife and a doctor's scalpel, the bread stolen by birds and the liquorice coins, the torment of an absence and the seven-league boots. Everything mingled without muddle under the clear maternal gaze. Sage face of silence. Quiet figure sitting beside a lamp, a study in light and shade. Through her attentiveness she was holding the world together till the end of time, and if there were lacerations too secret for her to heal, at least she bore witness to the unseen presence, which the worst of hurts could never drive away. We are without defence against our life. All we can do is welcome it, and listen to that second heart which is given to us, an earlier riser than the first. It borrows our body for a while and will outlive it, still beating to the measure of a prodigal time. Silence refreshes this imponderable heart, redder and more alive than life itself. Its nourishment is the unconsolable.

IV

It is a spring morning and I am walking with the lover along a country lane. This is a tale with nothing to tell, and it takes place long ago, although today is another spring morning, doubtless the same one behind the illusion of age and years. The lover is elusive and fleeting like her sisters the world over. She picks flowers of light by the armful, offers them me and takes them back, she melts into the day's brightness and returns, radiant and refreshed by a despair, graced by a peal of laughter, as changeful and wayward as only spring can be. I speak to her with a smile, as is proper with those one loves, of the clouds stretching out in the blue, of books lying exhausted to hand, or the featherweight hour in the sky: just the suggestion of a smile, to show that I'm not taken in by this clement disposition of things and stars, any more than by the waves of light that brush our temples and which, like everything else, will go into the dark, along with words and faces and hours. We are walking in a landscape that takes form under our feet and flight if one attempts to name it. I talk a little more and then fall silent. The dust on the road goes on dancing long after we have passed. The leaves on a hazel are trembling in the breeze: there is nothing so pure as the brightness of foliage, diffused in a thousand varicoloured glints. Nothing soothes more than the meekness of these tender leaves, utterly surrendered to the deluge of lights. Their speech is easy on the ear and shot through with silence.

Their being is transparent, open to the night as to the day; their submission draws on them a sheen of praise. To contemplate these leaves – whose vocation is to worship the source of their torment – purifies thought. As one's glance takes flight, nothing is left except these green, floating leaves, obedient to the whim of timeless currents and sustaining alone the whole weight of infinite space. We pursue our walk. One could walk a long time like this when the day is young. There are tufts of wool or horsehair caught on fences. There are nettles and white stones. And falling on all that, as on our lips, is the light of a spring morning. It comes and goes. It picks out nothing and celebrates all. It lends to our senses the purity of a skylark thrilling between an angel's fingers. Light: presence without flaw. It tells each grain of air, as children tally coming years and promised revels: *one, two, three, off to the woods go we: four, five, six, cherries we shall pick*. On goes the tale, the tale of this morning with nothing to tell, it doesn't end until – in the quiet withdrawal of evening – I wish to write about it: then the words grow faint and what they name is seen as from a great distance, like a fire catching in the face of sleep. Always there is a shadow, bent over the writer. Lover or god, it's all one. The shadow covers the whole page, takes up all the silence. She for whom one keeps watch with these few words merely passes through: she blows in with the wind and grabs a handful of fresh roses abandoned in the ink. Leaving the greeting on one's lips she whisks off, and all's to begin again. No rest, then, ever, never a last word, no end at all, in fact, to this matter of no importance: writing. One needs to invent a foreign language to address what is on its way and eludes one in the very process of its coming: the lover, the god or the light of a spring morning. How does one hold on to the grace of one day? It would take a language that was pure, ascetic. Sparing through abundance, closely attentive, it would listen sooner than speak. But words carry little weight. Keeping the eternal river within the bounds of its ink bed is beyond them. Where we are – in the eternal moment – there are no words, since everything is present. Where we are not – in the passing hour – only words are left, balled together like birds' down forgotten by the wind in rutted tracks. I write, it's a way of doing nothing. I am silent. I look at what is moving towards evening. How does one make a way through the triteness of all language, the night of each day? Help supervenes now and then. It comes unknown to us, and unknown too to the source that pours it out. It is given us by beauty that passes and dies in the passing. Like a space opened up by lightning. Like an island of light surrounded by black waters. It is the only succour we shall ever have, this beauty that lights our way while casting us into an even deeper night. I write, I do nothing. I love that life, so lacking in events. The withdrawal effects a clean sweep, and what can appear austere is simply the arrangement of everything that is – thoughts, fruits, inks – in view of the greatest possible abundance. I drink a coffee, to feel the cup burning my fingers. I look at a painting, to hear the silence. I wait, but not for waiting's sake. I am silent, I do nothing, and in an evening's nothing I slowly learn to name what fills me and eludes me: the wonder of a little green leaf astray in the rising flood of lights.

V

The big decisions are taken already in childhood, those that determine the course of the stars and the flow of dreams. They have their source in everything and nothing. They spring from the sudden revelation of the indigence of life in all its parts. At seven, the soul, already brought to term, lies curled round its own absence, like the petals of a rose lovingly folded round the inner void. The revelation of the abyss perfects it, adding the tang of a dark perfume which will infuse each day until the last. Thus does old age hurl its bolt right into childhood's playtime. A lightning knowledge leaving a glimmer that will last to the very end. These things stay muted. No tongue can bear to utter them and even the words used for wounding are too tender to bring them to the lips. This knowledge that all fails absolutely will take the child a long time to dilute in the bloodstream, burn in autumnal reading or disperse in the stress of a job. To grow up is to forget what one can't avoid knowing, and in which the child – for strength is given to it along with weakness – spends its waking hours: the disarray of words, the dereliction of all loves, and the slow debasement of dreams exposed to every wind. When or where this annunciation is made to the child matters little. It is enough that it takes place. A little earlier, a little later. Faced with the painful immediacy of such a thought, childhood turns inward for succour. The silence released by sadness finds a mute response in the silence of a decision – like a vow of madness taken under a dark star. The decision has no clear object. Indeed it has no substance other than silence. The azure of what is unsayable. The fierce will of a silence in which childhood takes refuge, determined to outlive itself within the parameters of what has just killed it. The light of such a wish is buried deep. It takes a long time to emerge into the day, years even: our childhood carries on, elsewhere. The scent of a summer garden, the moss on an old wall, the scarlet of a cherry tree take care of it. That someone is protecting us is obvious: we are so absent from our hours that it takes an angel to look after them, dusting the shadows on the sundial. For years I had no memory of my childhood. It merged with eternity and, like the latter, lay before me, pure, untouched. In this dazzlement I dreamed of the ancestral figures of whom I knew next to nothing: anecdotes, memories. Fictions secreted by the living round their grief, like a cocoon wound round a still open wound. Of one, my father would tell me that 'work wore him out', as when the flame blackens a wick, ruining the candle wax. A breath snuffed him. Of the other, a longtime resident of those asylums which have no door in any language, my mother spoke rarely, and then to say only that she was 'gentle, nice and liked her food'. That's all. I would never get to know any more, but, in fact, that exhausted all the knowledge I might ever have come by, about the living as well as the dead: a few approximations, never filled out. These people were absent from my early years. On the terrace of childhood only the sun was free to come and go. I think of them now and of that evil spell that bent the back of one and the mind of the other. That's how I see them, among so many others. Amid the injustice of the world, the harshness of a fate. They are there and not there. I am merely pursuing a path they were opening – he in his way, she in hers – without the chance of going further. One giving me my stubborn taste for idleness – that is, for love – the other that instinct for overreaching, which, far from compromising life, opens it to the eternal in an instant of utter beauty. Each bequeathing me what they lacked and what, by its absence, broke them. They are not there, and they are there. They return from time to time, to enjoy with me the mildness of the air. I know them no better than I know myself. It is with the infinity between us – like that between two strollers talking in the darkness – that I engage. In celebrating beauty, winter, light or books, it is that intimate part of themselves that I am celebrating, the intimacy of self with self, of which soul, and flesh likewise, were but a mirror image. 'What are you thinking about?' is what bores ask of someone communing dreamily with his origins. How do you say: I'm not thinking of anything. Not words or things. How do you say: I'm thinking about you, of what, in the centre of you, is the same as what's in the centre of me. I'm thinking about death and childhood. The one who is silent, who cannot answer, goes into the wood of a song where childhood is dead, where the bays are withered: *and if the cricket sleeps there, do it no harm*. He walks slowly in the strength that is eternal, keeping an equal distance from mastership and servitude. His only obedience now is to the flux of the stars in the blood, and he walks with a light step, as though evidence of loss were complemented by the evidence of salvation. As though the two silences – that of death swaddled in life and that of life winkled from death – had not always been one and the same, the silence of childhood in its boundless grief, in its eternal laughter.

VI

None can enter the chamber of death, any more than the chamber of delight, without at once changing name, and blood too. An angel stands in the doorway and it is not without trembling that we divine the shadow that touches him in the shoulder socket. Loving and dying proceed from the same knowledge, walk in step together. They are two brands that make a single fire, which is doubtless why we love so little and so badly: we should have to consent to our own defeat. We should have to lose and renounce everything, even what we had gained in the losing. It is only in love – in the gentleness of a hand, a slowness in the voice or the anguish in a look – that each thing recovers its place, its full place, in the perishable centre of itself: eternity is the element of the body that disintegrates fastest. Writing borrows from that twinned light a part of its radiance. The writer sees everything under an autumnal sun. He releases into the tenderest flesh as also into the simplest flower a dark knowledge that perfects them as it pulverises them. He traces the words of wisdom, the words of forgetting and calm. He applies himself. He hopes in so doing to ward off the coming of the night. He thinks he can hold out by presiding over the minutiae of his own obliteration. But it is no more than a game and a poor one at that. What is written doesn't hold. No form of words holds. The elation of finding the right word may, for a time, hearten us in this dream of power. But as the evening draws in, our lips pale and our sentences disappear into the dark – arrows lost in their invisible target. I look at the child who taught me all I know, Hélène. She steps into these pages, she is at home here. I see her dressed as a bride on the occasion of a fancy dress party at her school. I watch her dancing, lifted by a self-sustaining joy. She runs to the back of the hall, trailing a brightly coloured streamer like a ribbon of light in the wake of her laughter. By evening, her face is lit up with a fatigue that scatters her attention, now falling indifferently on all that meets her eye. The approach of sleep has left the face of the little six-year-old, in her dress dirtied with over-rich cake, so naked that I can see there, less than skin-deep, the dual infinity of her life and her death. I look at her and learn the painful knowledge that doesn't come in books: it is in exhaustion that we grow in strength. It is in surrender that princes are made, and in the blaze of dying that the full splendour of loving is revealed. If the beauty of a face is moving, it is thanks to this light that moulds it unaware – a brightness that merges with that of its future disappearance. All I have seen in the nobility of self-forgetful faces has been the traces of this radiance towards which each life is tending without knowing it: beauty and death keep up a ceaseless conversation in the open space of the face, like the subdued chatter of neighbours over the garden fence. The features of childhood – vowed by their perfection to a swift foundering – are sharper than all others. Their very freshness points to their loss. A child's face is a flower offered, promised to the scythe that gives it its brilliance, burning the ambient air. The end is present from the start, sometimes visibly. Then all one sees is the light that is secretly disfiguring the adored face. So do we divine our bourne and who is waiting for us. So too a face – next to nothing – imprints itself on us in the fleeting of its glory. Love of this nothing delivers us briefly from insignificance and then, very quickly, we forget. We turn back to the world. We forget the unforgettable: instinct, beauty. The dew of praise. We no longer see how like us all things are; how weak they are, like us; without support, like us; receiving everything full in the face, life, death, sprites and wolves. Like us. Forgotten the childhood prudence that taught us to dread bedtime and the end of paradise. Ears are deaf now to the anxious question at the heart of the oldest songs, begging for a little more time, a little more life: *Would that the rose were still on the tree, and that Pierre my dear friend still loved me.* We forget. We traipse off into the woods, we traipse off into the world which would be nothing at all if we didn't abet it by feeding, in our innermost depths, the dogs that are fighting over our white souls. Having renounced the highest knowledge – that of childhood – we have lost the force of clarity, the power of simplicity. We fail our lives. We fail everything. What is strange in fact is that grace still gets to us, when we do all we can to render ourselves unreachable. What is strange is that – thanks to a wait, a look, or a laugh – we sometimes gain access to that eighth day of the week, which neither dawns nor dies in the context of time. It is in the hope of such things that I live, and it is under that light that I write, savouring the beauty of each passing day. Writing is doubtless vain, and there is no guarantee that it prevents the night from coming, none whatsoever, but, after all, it can seem just as vain to love, sing or pick the first periwinkles – pale and tender as though emerging from a long illness – to bring them into the empty room. I look at them, I listen to what they teach: nothing opens as they do, save in the dark heart of idleness, save in a show of remorse for uselessness. I write, I don't write. I look at the child who is wandering off in her bridal gown, dazed with fatigue: child of the here-and-now, prey of the shadows. In the eternity of her gaze a single thought is left, white and weightless. She is falling, flying, going. On her own she fills heaven and earth, like those lime flowers that the breeze bears away, whirling on their own axis: dancing between air and air, they both offer and refuse themselves, never touching the ground. Hence the unique concept of a presence we would never again lack, of a beauty that would never again be subject to the outrages of evening, evil and death. To a child who asked me, 'what is beauty?' – and it could only be a child, for that is the only age that hankers after lightning and frets about what matters – I should answer: beauty is in all things that move away after once brushing our skin. Beauty is in the radical instability – a loss of balance and of voice – that the passing touch of a white wing provokes in us. Beauty is the sum of those things that pass through us, unaware of us, and suddenly intensifying the lightness of being. I would show the child the sky, where angels, wiping their hands on a cloud, create a Turner painting, and I would scoop up for him a handful of this earth that we are walking on. I would tell him that a book is like a song, that it's nothing, that it's for saying all that can't be said, and I would cut up an orange for him. We'd carry on walking late into the evening. In the silence we'd discover at last, he and I, the answer to his question. In the luminous vastness of a silence that words caress without disturbing it.

2

QUEEN, KING, JACK

This short piece might be described as a fairy tale for grown-ups. In a sense all fairy tales are for grown-ups, yet it is children who are their true interpreters. The dread lurking beneath the surface beauty, the silken lightness of this tripartite poem is better absorbed through the skin than pursued heavy-handedly with the blunt tools of language.

QUEEN, KING, JACK

Queen

As the sky dims to dusk the princess walks down the palace steps, crosses the garden where a few unicorns are playing, trails her fingers in the fountain of sweet wine and enters the hunting lodge with ivory doors. She sits down, collapses would be more exact, on the star-stuffed divan, worn out by the day to come. All have abandoned her, she is solitary without any consolation – the very thing that proves her a princess. For her sake, knights have performed the customary tests, killing the dragon, stealing a moon rose, capturing the ice bird. After which, they sought her hand from her father, the king, who received them graciously. And so they married her, but very soon their mouths were spitting fire, their eyes wandering and their hearts like ice. What they had overcome now triumphed over them in the most terrible trial of all, that of a trouble-free marriage. They went away again, dismissed in shame, and others came, pretending to the impossible. Under the paling sky, the princess re-arranges her hair with a comb of stuff-of-dreams. Tomorrow at dawn thirteen knights, vainglorious and agile, will climb on thirteen snow-white horses. They will ride to the confines of the kingdom, slay thirteen dragons, pluck thirteen blue roses and snare thirteen cold birds. The very thought makes her yawn and fatigue engulfs her as it does each evening:

expectation without hope, the bottle of black ink upset in the depths of the soul.

King

A king ages slowly, brightening his few remaining days with cruel entertainments, organising the odd massacre with a weary hand. Moment by moment favours or rages rain down on the kingdom, with all the melancholy of a thunderstorm sowing gold and blood among the wheat. One evening, in the instinctive way of animals fleeing an earthquake that they alone have felt, he leaves the palace by the back door and takes to the road, hoping to find a patch of earth where death won't nose him out. He walks through ruined villages, sleeps in burned-out barns, drinks from stagnant pools. The people he passes on his way have something strange about them. Be they children, old men or nurses, all have the same weak smile, the same far-off fixity of purpose in their eyes. Only after long wandering does he notice that all his subjects have, feature for feature, the same face as he: his kingdom is peopled entirely by himself. The horror of this discovery sends him homewards, only to learn on the way that the king has been dead thirty years and the palace is nothing more than a factory for pharmaceuticals. At that he turns away, covering his face with his hands, but behind the crossed fingers is a blank space, and the peasants gawp in wonder at a dummy on a mule, and the children make fun of the faceless scarecrow which holds no fear even for the sparrows.

Jack

Seated on a straw-bottomed chair the little tailor breaks a thread with his teeth, alters a hem, adjusts a shoulder seam. Well before the last star had died in the sky, he had been up and watching at his window for day to break, with an eye to the job on hand: a dress ordered by the queen, to be worn that very evening at the imperial ball. The messenger had mentioned a sizeable reward; moving the hot lantern above the sleepy face of the little tailor, he murmured that the punishment, in the case of default, would be immeasurably greater. He finally specified – shouting from the bridge leading out of the village – that the dress had to be cut from the light of that very day and no other stuff would do. Out of the pale tints of dawn the little tailor has already cut lilies, and waves like those of the sea, which he has stitched onto the noonday dazzle. He is just smoothing out the softer light of the afternoon, enough to make up a cape where every colour melts into the next. The needle flies through the air faster than seconds pass in the abyss, for there is no time to lose. From the red of the sunset he snips a wide russet sash, his ear attentive to the noise made by the queen's knights: from a point on the far horizon they are already nearing the village gates, and his frantic hand races to rival the speed of horses faster than forked lightning, as he vainly attempts to assemble a dress disintegrating in tatters and vanishing with the first shades of dusk.

3

LOOK AT ME, LOOK AT ME

This text and the following one ask to be looked at together. They first appeared in a collection of similar pieces entitled *Une petite robe de fête*, where the poet takes something lived or seen or read and lets it run, to truth by way of fairyland or vice versa. Except that it is of course tightly controlled, and therein lies the artistry. As always, the texts are layered. In 'Look at Me, Look at Me' Bobin speaks of 'the story of the Sundays', adding, 'but that is an eternal story', one he is 'barely able to write'. Both narratives are about little girls: in 'Look at Me', it is a child who is passionately in love with a fairground horse and lives for the Sundays when she gets to ride it. Parallel to this runs the thread of the battle with her parents over music practice. Bobin fosters the passion and sympathises with the rebellion. The merry-go-round of life continues, leaving the poet sidelined, yet wiser, like the child.

In 'Get Moving, Jonah, I'm Waiting', the children are more peripheral. The writer looks on as two ten-year-old girls, temporary fugitives from the new estate with its lookalike villas, play in the waste ground left by the bulldozers. They themselves are the playthings of the gale that blows across the treeless expanse, yet its playmates, too, as they laugh at its unbridled strength. Their parents, meanwhile, suffocate in a dust-cloud of cement and money. The wind and the spirit, that both blow where they will, lead the reader into another world, another gale and another story, that of Jonah, sent to announce God's judgement to the get-rich-quick of an earlier city. This is a tale of many-faceted repentance, ending with the God-wind – or wind-god – bowing down and 'laughing madly before two ten-year-old children', the only ones who have nothing to repent of.

These texts give up their riches when read as poetry: not only has every word been considered, chosen and placed, even the pattern on the page contributes to the meaning. The flow is uninterrupted from start to finish: no paragraphs, one long rectangle of black on white broken by page breaks. Full stops command. Childhood's shifting attention gets short sentences: ten words, or three. Staccato. In the second, wind, sea and spirit are given leeway in sentences that stretch out to accommodate the wildness of the gale, the swell and suck of the sea. By the time a lower case god comes on the scene, the process is advanced: Jonah and the narrator tell the story in five sentences that snake sinuously down the page, their segments held in place by commas.

LOOK AT ME, LOOK AT ME

She rings you every Sunday. Sunday is her favourite day
– the day she goes to meet with a little white horse,
a skittish one. He's in the stable, apart. Away from
the others that he can't endure. A miniature horse. A
snowy horse, hot-blooded. She could choose other
ones. She has eyes for him alone. Child and horse get
on famously. The little horse is a speed fanatic. He's
been known to anticipate his rider's wishes. He bolts on
the roundabout, does just as he pleases. He's the horse
you dream of: shiny with sweat, lit up with impatience.
The little girl loves him like a brother. Or a second self.
Seeing them together brings a smile. They seem made
for each other, born on the same day. In this horse the
child meets with the part of her that is most alive – her
wild part, her lunar, stormy side. Each Sunday she learns
about herself, through fear and play. There is nothing
else to learn about in life but oneself. There's nothing
else to be known. Of course, one doesn't learn on one's
own. One's secret depths are only reached through
another. Through a love, through a word or a face. Or
through a little white horse. When the lesson ends the
afternoon has scarcely begun. Other lessons follow, less
enjoyable. Homework not yet done. And the trying
obligation to sit at the black piano, as on every other day.
Regretfully she leaves the white horse. Each time it's
the everlasting question, the dark enigma: why can't we
stay here? Since I'm happy here. Since when I'm with

the white horse I'm closest to me. So why do I have to move on, carry on, what's the point of all those hours that take me away from me and everything else? You don't know what to answer. You cannot answer since, like her, you have always discovered life through play – and nowhere else. You take her home in silence. She has her tea and chatters as the day draws in. She goes to the piano only after many calls and a lot of shouting. In the depths of despair. It's the same drama every time, the drama of parents and child: the two who map out a steady onward path, the one who hares off into the countryside. The two who walk and the one who dances. Sometimes the parents bicker. You let her do whatever she wants. She'll never get anywhere, that child. She seizes the occasion to run away. Sometimes they team up, and together prove too forceful and too strident: she comes to sit on the piano stool. Slowly. Negotiating her surrender to the end, to the last gasp, the moment when she presses down the white and black keys. Hesitantly to begin with. As though her fingers had a stammer. The river flows in straight lines across the score. The limpid waters of clear melody. The child has to reach the river in front of her. Miles away to begin with. The distance between page and hand, self and self, is frightening. Or would be frightening if all were not given, perfect, directly the first key is pressed down. There's weakness at the start. Towards the end there's grace. In between come a necessary growth of understanding and the detour through effort and duration. Beginning and ending are given together, but this is seen only later. Much, much later we see that there was never any difference between the maladroit child and the deftness of the god, between flower and fruit. Grace does not rid us of our blunderings: it crowns them. Two uncertain notes and the music is already there, radiant. Achieved in those shaky beginnings. After that, it's simple; a mere matter of learning, of letting the music come to you. Gently. A little closer each day. Taming the golden horse of music. Feeding him with your fingers. You look at the child's back, bent over the keyboard. The hard grind of getting to know oneself, coming to grips with what one doesn't know – well beyond the fenced paddocks and the sheet music. What does it mean, to learn. Learning to play, learning to live. What is it, other than this: to lay a finger on what is most elemental in ourselves. On the most vital and rebellious. Weeks go by and turn to months. She doesn't bother to ring you any more: it's understood that Sundays are for you and for the horse. You meet her there. You watch her while you smoke a cigarette. Eight or ten children on horses, and this one, the one that counts, on her snow-white mount, her face radiating light. You are besotted with adoration. You are in fact more and more inclined that way with every face you see. Writing is no help, it tends rather to increase the stupor, this seizure of the world by removing oneself. As you stand by the roundabout, thoughts are circling through your mind, but none interferes with your view of the horses ambling round, each with its own character and name. She, the child, likes you to be there, looking at her. When she was playing she would sometimes utter the cry all children voice, what earth wants from sky and the sky from the earth, the universal plea, that sudden escape of truth: look at me, look at me! It's what children call out at the most perilous moment of a game, the moment of anticipated honour and glory. Look at me, look at me! Horses want that too, you say to yourself, and so do trees, and the mad and the poor, and everything that lives – for a time – in time. Here, there and everywhere the same call, the same appetite for the glory of being loved, recognised; everywhere the yearning of the exiled and their hunger for the heart's true home – in the eyes of another. Look at me, look at me! Such are your thoughts in front of the roundabout, mixed in with others: the rent to be paid, the page to be written, the shoes that need mending. What's in your head is similar to what's before your eyes: without bounds or focus. Time moves on again, leaving Sundays untouched. A year, two years. The piano has vanished. It's still there, but the child never goes to it. She has struck a bargain. Look: I'm playing two instruments, the flute and the piano. That's one too many. I'll give up the black tomb of the piano and carry on with the living water of the flute. Every day, promise. In exchange there's to be one Sunday a week, with a horse in the middle of it. She keeps her promise. The music session becomes less stormy. There's still a threat of thunder in the voices, the parents huff and puff a bit, but it's all right really, getting better and better. She plays the flute superbly. No strings, no ivories, no stool. Only the air, a reed of air between the fingers. The flute is better – goes better with the little horse. The piano's a bit recent, a latter-day invention, like reading or happiness. There haven't always been pianos, reading or happiness in the world. There have always been horses, fairies and wind in the reeds, always, right from the beginning, ever since god was born on the steppes of Asia, in the giant forests and on the green water of the lakes. Sunday follows Sunday, keeping to the same clear arrangement: first the horse, then the flute. Last come bath, meal and bed. It has been going on now for three years. The child will grow older, as you are well aware. One day you'll see her less often, and then hardly at all. One day the white horse will be laid to sleep in a black field – blacker than the piano. You know that too. But it won't affect the story of the Sundays. That is an eternal story, one you are barely able to write. Yes, everything will change: the child, the horse and you yourself. Everything except the light, the beautiful light of those Sundays, and the voice it proceeds from, a voice radiant from lack of everything – the gallop of a hot little horse over the naked voice, in the white heart: look at me, look at me.

4

GET MOVING, JONAH,
I'M WAITING

GET MOVING, JONAH, I'M WAITING

The two girls are walking ahead of you. They are ten years old. They are walking across the dead land beyond the villas. The wind is tangling their hair, undoing their talk. The wind has come from the ocean and has swept masterfully over hundreds of towns and roads, bending trees, uprooting fences, banging shutters, and loosing its full strength here, on the faces of two children, two friends in the kingdom of their ten years. The wind has had to deploy much cunning, and much love and patience to find them there; it has scoured the surroundings of the shivering villas and pursued them as far as this waste ground. They don't usually come here, they aren't used to walking on this ocean of red soil. A clay soil, gouged out by excavators, searched through by thunderstorms, a remnant of infinity. Hills the height of children, pits as deep as their games. In front of you the two girls, nearly choking with laughter because the wind is squeezing them so. Behind you, the knee-high walls edging the residences, the domestic desert. The villas are lookalikes. Same stone, same roofs, same green gardens – a caged green, the grass well behaved. The estate is the property of the bank. Confident executives have sold every plot. Smiling sales girls have trotted out the details: space, light, amenities. Young couples have studied the plans, giving as much attention to the attribution of the rooms as to the name of the baby on the way. My desk in this corner, the children upstairs and despondency throughout. The villas sprang up in the course of a summer. They grew as one sometimes wishes children might grow: unflawed, problem-free, lifeless. It was afterwards that the rain came. An invisible rain, a dust-cloud of cement and money, in the new rooms an air that stifled, a loan with twenty years to run. The roads between the villas bear the names of flowers or writers. A counterfeit coinage, old frocks dressed up. The children go from name to name, cross barriers, scatter at dinnertime, come back at nightfall, sit in the roadway, circulate everywhere, flocks of birds on dry land. Neither banks nor the tedium of living to repay the banks can ever stop childhood from spending its gold – without counting. The two girls carry on across the waste ground, from time to time the wind is too strong and they turn faces shining with cold and joy in your direction. This single face becomes an enigma as you look. It bears a name which isn't just that of the children, it's the name too of that waste land abandoned by the architects, the young couples, the bankers – abandoned by all except the wind. A name unlike the street names, a name the wind murmurs to you later, much later in the waste land of your reading, under the cloak of that book of god's despair – the Bible, an ocean of red utterance. The first knowledge we acquire of god is bitter and sweet, gulped in with the earliest nutriments of childhood. A child licks god, drinks him, hits him, smiles at him, shouts at him and ends up sleeping in his arms, replete in the nook of the dark. This knowledge is immediate, offered to the new-born, denied to the clerical establishment, denied to those whose knowledge of god is thin – a knowing cut off from its known. Your way of reading the Bible is miles away from theirs: one sentence, maybe two, no more. It isn't easy to read in a storm. You can't read more than a line or two in these pages racked by the wind, tormented by the draught of an absence preferable to anything beside. Reading the Bible is at one extreme of your life as a reader, in this life beneath the ruins. At the other extreme is the newspaper. The newspaper as reading is black, thick, static. The Bible as reading is white, luminous, flowing. In the newspaper everything gets read since nothing is essential. You proceed methodically from the faces of ministers to the legs of athletes, from South America to the farthest end of China, from the rate of the dollar to the unemployment figures. Reading the paper is a serious matter, and like all serious matters has no bearing on life. You read a single sentence in the Bible and it's like a drop of neat alcohol, an angel's tear. You open the book, set your finger at random on the page, it lights on a fish, a palm tree, a lamb, you read, you move from your life to life, from the simple present to the present super-perfect. In the Bible there is god, and indeed there is none but he. He speaks without pause. In many words and none, in lightning bolts and the breeze of an airy April morning, in the rustle of standing wheat and the ox's exhalation, in the white curl of a wave and a tongue of flame – he speaks in everything the world contains. In the Bible god speaks to god, without drawing breath, in a voice now furious, now smiling, now gentle with anger, now hoarse from so much shouting. In the Bible god is sick of talking to god and not being heard, and yet he goes on calling, calling … such loneliness, such love, it's unthinkable, touch the book and your thought falls apart, only your eyes left to read and burn: how can one be so lonely and not die of it, how be so long a-dying and still be there, such strength wasted since the day of creation, so much love – how can it be? In the Bible the wind is talking to the wind, the wind tells stories to itself so it shan't feel too alone, the wind of god on the lake of a voice, the wind that moves on the waters, the wind that enters the houses, god the wind, the breath that is god. One day he says to Jonah, Jonah, you're to go to the people of this city, you must tell them I can't stand them any longer, that my heart is very heavy, my blood very dark, you will announce their coming death, get moving, Jonah, I'm waiting. And Jonah doesn't want to be the bearer of that kind of message, and Jonah doesn't want to give heart-room to a thunderbolt, so he boards a ship, he wants to flee god, he knows it isn't possible but he tries, at least he will have tried, and out at sea the wind gets up and the ship labours in the maddened seas, the sailors say, there's someone here who's got all the dogs of death on his heels, which means on ours, we've got to get rid of him, he'll have to go overboard now, that chap. Jonah tells his story, says that he doesn't want to keep his promise, the promise god is making to god that everything will get wiped out, and the sailors throw Jonah overboard and a whale that happened to be passing swallows Jonah all the way into its belly, the world's black hole, where he stays three days and three nights. While he's in the whale Jonah sings, there's nothing to do except sing in the dark, the cavernous belly of the dark, in the end he says right, you win, I give in, I'll go there, I'll tell these people of your anger and their doom. And when he has delivered his message, when he has told the people of this town: you are lost, so lost that you don't know any longer how lost you are, I've come to proclaim it to you, it is the wind speaking to you through my voice, the wind which is coming tomorrow to demolish your villas, your banks, your sad happinesses and your cinder gardens, when Jonah has spat out all these words he goes off quietly, pleased with himself, he has done his job. The people believe this news, they think it's all up with us, god won't revoke his decision, this time it's the end, and with that they shut down their computers, leave their offices and go into the street to take their place in the day with no tomorrow, that is to say the grace of living, which is to say god. And here, now, comes the best bit, which lies, as throughout the Bible, in god's inconsequence, in the weakness of a god who lets himself be melted by the surrender of these people, a god who rescinds his decree, a foolish god who contradicts the sensible, the wise god – just as one sees the wind suddenly hesitate, turn right back on its course, take in its hands the faces of two girls, only to give way before this fullness of light and childhood, and, suddenly putting off all its violence, retain only the gentleness of its strength, saying there is something stronger than I, stronger than the thunder god, holier than the lightning god, and bow down – bow down laughing madly before two ten-year-old children wandering on a piece of dead land, Jonah place, residence of the whales.

5

A WORLD OF DISTANCE

The title given to this text – *L'Éloignement du monde* – is a clear pointer to its theme, but with Bobin the clear is rarely simple and never obvious. The two main words in their relation to each other are dense with an ambiguity impossible to bring out fully in English. Is it the world that is receding here? Or is a hidden subject withdrawing from the world? The first paragraph, quoted below, unwraps the poet's thought a little further: a reader may conclude that it is less a case of 'either … or', than of 'and … and'. Ultimately agency is shown as resting with the individual: the world may indeed withdraw to a distance, but will do so only in a given context, when inner space is made for its replacement (silence, solitude – types of the eternal), and with love as the necessary medium:

> If we consider our life in relation to the world, we need to resist what others would make of us, refuse whatever presents itself – roles, identities, functions – and defend above all else our silence and our solitude. If we consider our life in its relation to eternity, we need to relax our grip and accept what

comes, holding on to nothing. Rejecting all on the one hand, accepting all on the other: this double movement can take place only within the love in which the world retreats while the eternal draws closer, solitary and silent.

Below the literal, under the metaphorical can be heard the muted dialogue of free will and grace: the poet who a few years later will see 'God blowing past the sitting room window ... disguised as a small yellow leaf', and, in the very personal text *Le Christ aux coquelicots*, will affirm: 'I need your light to write by', is here still keeping his distance.

The piece is unusual in being a virtually unpeopled text (three unnamed and unlocated recipients of 'letters' have disappeared in this abbreviated version): the beloved alone slips in from time to time; she is 'the air that never fails' and cannot be kept out. *A World of Distance* is the closest Bobin gets to abstract writing. The finely crafted reflections, exploring and developing the theme set out at the start, stand confidently on their own. It is only at the close that readers find themselves invited to join Bobin in his favourite place – his personal world – the pool of Saint-Sernin in Saône-et-Loire.

A WORLD OF DISTANCE

There were times when a long sword of silence would penetrate my heart. Pulling it out would have brought on an immediate haemorrhage: all that was left to me was to keep silent and write sentences like this where the white rules. Each one was liberating for me at the moment of its coming. I have never written except to resolve a crisis, make my way through a forest, or back to the clear weather under a louring sky. I have never written save for you and me, a 'you' and a 'me' to come, not yet present in this world where there has never yet been anyone at all.

If we consider our life in relation to the world, we need to resist what others would make of us, refuse whatever presents itself – roles, identities, functions – and defend above all else our silence and our solitude. If we consider our life in its relation to eternity, we need to relax our grip and accept what comes, holding on to nothing. Rejecting all on the one hand, accepting all on the other: this double movement can take place only within the love in which the world retreats while the eternal draws closer, solitary and silent.

All that we do consists only of waiting, and the dross of wants and cravings we place between us and our expectation is nothing but the product of our impatience.

From the perspective of the spirit, there is no distinction between excess and dearth: the more one frequents solitude, the more one needs it. The more we are plunged in love the more we feel its lack. We shall never have enough solitude and the same is true of love, that sheer slope of solitude.

Weariness is like a stone inside us. If a single heave could lift it, we should discover what lies beneath, which is paradise.

Love is detachment, forgetfulness of self. We cannot arrive at it unaided, for our whole strength is ceaselessly employed in heaping the world on the surface of our ego. What we take at times for detachment is merely indifference or resignation – just two more metamorphoses of the ego, buttressed in the case of indifference, darkened in resignation.

The wind buffets foliage in the way a declaration affects the face of a woman in love, arousing the same grace of surrender, the same radiant excitement. Wind and word speak the same language of love.

If we went about the world as relaxed as a child who falls asleep in the thick of a crowd, the world would have no more power to trouble our hearts than to weigh on the light and unimpeded breathing of the sleeping child.

The wretchedness so evident in our relationships is not the fault of love. We'd do better to ask ourselves what makes it so hard for us to love others without tying them at once to our own fate, which comes back to asking why we find it so hard to love.

*

Little tree rustling with light, to see you gives me the same lift as seeing the beloved in the dress she bought for a song.

Certain things take flight as soon as we start to wait for them. Calling them is a waste of time: however soft our voices, all they hear is our craving and they withdraw from us as far as they can, into themselves, where we can no longer hurt them.

A child at play gives out more light in its playing than saints at their prayers or angels singing. The playing child is the consolation of God.

Light indeed the bird that doesn't need to own the forest in order to sing, not even a single tree.

Today, my love, I am too tired to write to you. You will find in your heart a letter several pages long, filled with silence. Read it slowly. Today's light wrote it in my name. It is all about you and the quiet that fills me whenever I turn my face to yours, there where you are, all those miles away.

The certainty of having, just once, for a day, been loved marks the *definitive* flight of the heart into the light.

*

Every action, even the most ordinary, especially the most ordinary – opening a door, writing a letter, extending a hand – should be performed with the greatest care and the liveliest attention, as if the fate of the world and the course of the stars hung on them – anyway, the fate of the world and the course of the stars do hang on them.

We send our shadow on an embassy, far ahead of us. We watch it talking to other shadows, shaking hands with them and sometimes coming to blows. We observe all that from a distance and reality plays little part in our lives – until some joy or grief breaks in which we start by refusing to believe in.

The natural principle that separates each life from every other has been dismantled in themselves by the saints till nothing in the universe is alien to them: their hearts vibrate alike to the singing of a star and the murmur of the snow, to the smiles of the dead and the wails of the newly born. There is no humanity other than the saints' humanity: none that cannot be defined as supernaturally besotted, besottedly supernatural.

*

Marvelling creates in us an indraught. Eternity sweeps at the speed of light into a space suddenly emptied of everything.

A sleeping child is the image of eternal life, surrendered trusting into the hands of God. The tremulous tree is the image of ephemeral life, subject to the seasons' moods. The child that sleeps and the tree that trembles are the two supreme images of living life.

I know nothing, my love, to rival in glory your face when you laugh. Death, which will take all the rest, won't succeed in capturing the light of your face within me. It will take the rest for having already held it in its arms in my lifetime. It will fail to take this face though, and would burn its fingers if it even approached it.

We pass our lives outside a door without seeing that it stands wide open and that what lies behind it is right there, before our eyes.

Flux of passing light, wave of living light, beauty of these lights that plumb the sky and glide on the waters, enigma of this impassible beauty, careless of our fate: I have never seen such splendour as in the sky of Poland, a few kilometres from the concentration camp of Treblinka.

*

The little child ventures into language as one explores a foreign country: picking up certain intonations, quick to learn the rudiments necessary to satisfy basic needs. Our so-called native language is just a foreign tongue that we have, over time, thoroughly assimilated. The only language that is genuinely native is the one whose every subtlety is known to us, unlearnt: faces are its words. Its sentences are those of a love that leaves no whit of us on foreign soil.

The spoken word is *never* heard exactly as it's said: once we have accepted that, we can move around at ease in speech, wholly unconcerned with being understood, careful only to keep our speech as close as possible to our lives.

We go this way and that in search of a joy crumbled and dispersed. A sparrow's hop is our only chance of tasting God scattered on the ground.

What can be hoped for from a pure love other than a purified solitude?

There is a thickness between life and us. Call it fatigue, fear, thought, ambition, or all of these – each will be correct, but the all-embracing name is: ourselves. It is we, the seeming obstacle that stands between our life and us, the thickening of our selves within us that we consider a proof of maturity, confirming our existence. We should instead be wandering through our lives as though we were no longer there, with the litheness of a cat in the long grass or the quiet smile of a woman in love looking at her rifled heart.

To write is to give extreme care to what we are doing – something impossible in life where we focus on the essential while neglecting the rest, forgetting that the essential is nothing else than what we neglect.

*

The world holds together only because we believe ourselves bound to carry it on our shoulders – without seeing that no one is asking us to do such a thing.

I have found, my love, the most secret and the clearest name to spell out the meaning of your life in mine: air. You are the air that never fails, that air indispensible for thought and laughter, the air that refreshes my heart and turns my solitude into a place open to the four winds.

Solitude is one of the principal goods of life, on a par with food and sleep. The dailiness of our need of these goods dispenses us from all other justification: there is no more call on us to justify the need to be alone than to argue the need for food and sleep.

In the eyes of the world the powerful hold the highest place. In the eyes of the spirit they occupy the lowest and evoke only the compassion felt in the face of grave infirmities.

We complain of the world as we might complain of being unable to leave a room after locking the door and tossing the key through the window.

A lofty self-awareness goes hand in hand with an inwardly depressive state – as an empire that has lost its self-belief fortifies its frontiers and takes a pride in its tombs.

Love lets us reach out to the lost heart of the world with infinite tact and sensitivity, as in a dream in which we see a door that opens before us in response to our mere intention, before we have laid a hand on the knob.

*

Irony is a symptom of avarice, a contraction of the intelligence, which clenches its teeth sooner than let slip a single word of praise. Humour, inversely, is a sign of generosity: smiling at what one loves is to love it twice as much.

Writing is a strange pursuit, seeing that it is less a pursuit than a state and less a state than the hope of a state of fulfilment, which, if we could attain it and remain there indefinitely, would dispense us from writing.

Just as the child, learning to walk, leans on its mother's body as on something felt to be immovably solid, so should we, on our way through the world, lean on our inner and unshakeable solitude.

The thing we call 'me' and hold so dear is similar to a snowflake colliding with thousands of its kind in a struggle both perilous and frighteningly short.

— How long have you been writing?
— Since writing ceased to be my object.

The saints know of a door between the world and love. If they pass through it in silence it is because this door and their silence are one.

There isn't a 'problem' of Evil, for a problem always implies the hope of a solution. There is a light of Evil, which is unequalled, except by the light of Good. The first leaves the eternal blinded and, for a time, in retreat. The second blinds the world.

*

Our ignorance of life's hidden depths does not prevent us from living it and thereby acquiring an understanding of it that is *perfect*, even if inarticulate.

— You speak too much of love.
— Name one thing, just one, that is not connected
with love and is worth three seconds of speech.

Holiness is so far from perfection as to be its polar
opposite. Perfection is the spoilt little sister of death.
Holiness is a potent taste for life as it goes – a childlike
capacity to rejoice in what is, without asking for anything
else.

We need to guard, not only against the world, but against
our preoccupation with ourselves, another door by
which the world might creep back into us like a prowler
into a sleeping house.

Beauty heals the spirit by aggravating its ailment – salt
thrown on an open wound.

It is the fever of a rosebush after a shower that best
resembles what we term 'the inner life': we receive our
souls only from *without*, like a gift that surprises us each
time.

The living are few and the dead abound in this life – the
dead being those who never let go and can't walk away
from themselves into love or laughter.

Prayer is our one link with the real – if by 'prayer' we
mean simply an attention both extreme and careless
of any result, an attention so pure that the one who
practises it is not even aware of doing so.

Peaceful pool of Saint-Sernin in Saône-et-Loire, I think of you this evening, wishing that my ink might be as vibrant as your waters trodden by the bare feet of the angels, and that the light you dispense without measure might be found in the reading of this little book.

6

MOZART AND THE RAIN

This is a piece about beginnings and endings. It opens with the new-born Bobin, closely shawled, introduced to the wet of an April snow shower. 'Today when I go out into the street and rain runs down my face, I re-learn being born, I go back to the beginning, to that first encounter with the mortal side of life. A mortality that refreshes. Like Mozart. Just like Mozart.' It ends with Mozart's burial and a reflection on silence.

Between beginning and end is strung a series of vignettes in most of which Bobin figures as observer or actor. Each follows the same movement from the particular to the general, from something seen or experienced to the light which that experience throws on human mortality, while the focus shifts from birth towards the greater existential question of death. Bearing in mind its title, the text might be seen as a composition, with Mozart supplying the *leitmotif*, the rain an intermittent descant – Bobin is a great lover of both. As presented to us, the listening world, Bobin is not only the conductor and the principal player in this performance, he is also the chorus, commenting, interpreting – a filter for joy and suffering.

MOZART AND THE RAIN

White and weightless.

My first experience of life was white and weightless. I have often heard it pictured for me by my mother. She is coming out of the maternity clinic carrying me in her arms. We are right at the end of April, but it is snowing nonetheless. In my mind's eye it is the wet of the flakes I am aware of first, rather than their brightness or their dancing. The rain element. Whatever one does to shield a new-born baby from bad weather, by swaddling it in blankets and holding it close, the out-of-doors still comes to meet it – the air, the happiness of wet invigorating air. I am alive because I was spoken to and loved. I am alive because, in my very first hours, my mother and the rain aspect of snow spoke to me with love. Today when I go out into the street and rain runs down my face, I re-learn being born, I go back to the beginning, to that first encounter with the mortal side of life. A mortality that refreshes. Like Mozart. Just like Mozart.

There is a lot of suffering in the world, and, in equal quantity, a lot of childhood. These two things are one and the same. For the world, the spirit of childhood is unbearable. It has to abandon childhood in order to carry on being world. What we abandon doesn't die, but wanders abroad and finds no rest. Grief keeps it company. To this unsleeping childhood both Mozart and the rain know just what to say and how to say it, in a voice that is near and low, a simple, mothering voice.

My relationship with Mozart is very similar to my relationship with L. My first conversation with L. took place in the dark. Between L. and me, an ocean and a time lag of six hours. Words flew, limpid, from my night to her day. Talk spans oceans. Since that day – or that night, depending on which side of the ocean one happens to be – L. has been there, dancing around in my life in company with Mozart and everyone I love. I never see L. and I rarely listen to Mozart. No matter: seconds suffice to re-establish conversation, to bridge an ocean. We are not masters of our ways of loving. They take root very early and stay put. My way of loving lies in letting go and letting be. L. has just completed a long tour of America in a giant bus. She tells me in a letter how she wishes she could find in books as many miracles as on these trips where nothing happens. I don't know whether L. and I will meet one day before we each die our own death. I don't know what I think about death. I'm not sure the mind can encompass something so delicate and abrupt, comparable to a spring rain stripping the cherry blossom.

*

Sweetness, grace, charm: words describing Mozart's style that have been over-used. They have no energy left. I leave them lying to grab hold of another, better suited: clarity. The greatest gift we can be given in this murky life is clarity – even when clarity, as happens, kills us.

Neither too much silence, nor too little: the patter of raindrops on the leaves of the plane tree and the twitter of swallows skimming Mozart's scores are good tutors in the nice use of language.

Everything has its opposite, the conjoined other with which it wrestles and dialogues. For me the dark counterpart to Mozart's music is the tocsin that rang out on the day of your funeral: the void vibrating in the overheated air of August 1995. On the one hand the booming of the bronze, repeating the only phrase it knows. On the other the passion of a musician who multiplies notes – to say what, exactly: next to nothing, the opposite of the tocsin. The two phrases are of course inseparable. One dark, the other light, the one digging, the other dancing. Inseparable, as are true enemies.

Something happened on the evening of your death. Many things happened that evening. While you were wrestling with shadows, I was looking after your little daughter. The time came to put her to bed. She didn't know you wouldn't be coming back. At four years old, she was still used to your getting her a bottle. I warmed the milk, sprinkled in the chocolate-flavoured powder and shook the bottle to mix it. She watched me, at first disbelieving, then derisive: you don't do it like that, she said. She took the bottle out of my hands and showed me the proper way: I shouldn't shake the bottle, but simply roll it between my palms, as though I was rubbing them together to warm them after bitter cold. In the child's gesture it was yours I saw – your way of looking after those you love, the trouble you take over trifles. I am morbidly alert to details of this sort. Nothing in life moves me more deeply than these little gestures, basic yet indispensible if day is to follow day. My masters are musicians, poets, painters, mages. My masters are little children. They teach me the proper way of mixing milk and flavouring, desire and expectation, a grief with a musical note, a laugh with the note that follows.

Between myself and the world, a pane of glass. Writing is a way of passing through without breaking it.

*

My mother's final gestures in the preparation of a meal are invariably attended by mishap. She cooks to perfection. With her, catastrophe strikes as she is dishing up. At the last minute, while she's setting the dish on the table or spooning food onto a plate, something catches, splashes or gets spilled. Slightly. But surely. As though, from behind the diligent care given to her family a hint of impatience poked its nose: I've spent hours in the kitchen for your sakes, but now, if you don't mind, I'm off on holiday, I'm not that focused on what I'm doing, for a fraction of a second I'm stepping down from my sovereign status of servant, do you really think that's what I'm made for? I love this last-minute break-out, this unacknowledged flitting. There is such a thing as a fostering impatience. In Mozart too one can stumble on facile last-minute solutions and botched ends of movements. They add to the beauty of the whole. Women who send their nearest packing, musicians who dispatch the last three notes, imps who recite the life-sustaining prayer: 'My God, protect us from perfection, deliver us from any such desire.'

*

From time to time I lose the rhythm which has always suited me, a rhythm in two-time, presence–absence, speech–silence, and I am left with only one of these states, which has me endlessly falling: an unlistening chatter, a silence of refusal – nothing but wrong notes.

Beauty takes us in her arms and carries us for a few moments level with her face, just as mothers do with their little ones when they wish to kiss them, and then, without warning, she puts us down, back in our bumbling lives – just as mothers do.

Words and music, I eat both of them – but lack and absence are my basic foods, the primary ones.

*

Melancholy is up each morning one minute before me. Like someone stealing my light, it stands between the window and me. Just to wake up, I have to manhandle it aside. Melancholy loves death, deeply. For years now I have been wrestling with these depths, striving to limit their influence and not always managing. Only the lightness of life can drive out a melancholy deeper than a plumb line. Lightness has always come to me from the direction of love. Not sentiment, love. It took me a long time to work out what separated love from sentiment: almost nothing, an abyss. Sentiment is close to melancholy and sooner or later will slide into it. Sentiment and melancholy spring from a preference of self for self, a complaisance – heightened or hopeless – of me for me. Sentiment and melancholy are equally unfathomable, full of nooks and eddies. Melancholy is the dark face of the sentimental. Sentiment, like melancholy, clings, fetters, fuses. Love cuts, detaches, flies. Sentiment, like birdlime, glues my self within me. By love I am detached from it, torn free. There is in

Mozart and the Rain

Mozart's music a militant, active love. He answers the question I put to myself daily on waking: how do I get into this first morning of the world?

*

I should like to know how to pray, I should like to know how to cry for help, how to thank, how to wait, how to love, how to weep, I should like to know what can't be learnt, but I know none of it, all I know is how to sit and let God in to do the work for me, God or more often, for one mustn't be demanding, one of his go-betweens, rain, snow, the laughter of children, Mozart.

The most luminous moments in my life are those where I am content to watch the world appearing. These moments are made up of solitude and silence. I am stretched on a bed, sitting at a desk or walking in the street. I have left yesterday behind and tomorrow doesn't exist. Every personal bond is loosed, yet no one is a stranger to me. This experience is simple. It is not a matter of wanting it. It is enough to receive it when it comes. One day you lie down, sit or walk, and everything comes easily to meet you, no more need to choose, all that comes bears the mark of love. Maybe even solitude and silence can be dispensed with as preludes to these moments of surpassing purity. Love alone would be enough. What I am describing is a modest experience anyone may have – for example, in those moments when, without a thought in one's head, forgetful even of one's own existence, one presses a cheek against a cold window-pane to watch the rain falling.

*

The frequently troubled lives of the creative impress me less than those of the poor. It takes as much genius – in the way of courage, dreams, patience and impatience, innocence and ruse – to find the rent money and clothe the children as to put together a masterpiece.

Mozart's funeral – the dog trotting behind the hearse, the body buried in a pauper's grave: if my compassion goes out to the dead Mozart it is to the empty man, not to the artist. When death comes there are no artists any more, just little children pushed out into the dark.

Plunge your hands in the river. Watch the water brought up against this unforeseen check, and how cheerfully it finds a way round it. Let the coolness mount from hands to soul. Squatting there vacantly, like a child in front of a cricket, listen to the water running by, the limpid insolence of time flying: you have just felt, seen and heard a Mozart sonata for violin and piano.

Mozart and the Rain

Between earth and sky, a ladder. At the top of this ladder, silence. Speech and writing, however persuasive, are no more than rungs. The foot should be placed on them only lightly, without pressure. Speaking, sooner or later, turns to showing off. Writing, sooner or later, turns to showing off. At one point or another. Inevitably. Perforce. Silence alone is never sly. Silence is first and last. Silence is love – and when it is not, it is more wretched than noise.

It is the silent hours whose song is the purest.

THE TIGHTROPE WALKER

Not quite a fairy tale, more a fantasy. This is Christian Bobin talking to himself, or rather to his alter ego, the man with a horse's head, whom he spots one day in a field while out walking. They strike up a friendship, having, after all, a lot in common. The narrator has just lost his job, to his relief, and is now engaged in lobbing stones into ditches. The tightrope walker has lost his beloved, who had a mare's head and shared his double act in the circus. Unemployed, he too is waiting, but for what? A space is made for the reader in their conversation. The tightrope walker, who is something of a poet, tells his story of love and loss, of joy and pain, which takes only the time for his mane to turn white and the talk to rheumatism. One day in this timeless tale a life-changing discovery is made by the horse-headed friend and shared over a basket of apples. The following morning the narrator, arriving with replenishments, finds the field empty. He goes home and finds his house changed too – for good. The fable-like simplicity of the tale, the deceptive simplicity of the dialogue are layers for the reader to peel back. Behind them lies, not an allegory, which Bobin always shuns, but a landscape of divergent paths waiting to be explored.

THE TIGHTROPE WALKER

The first time I met the man with the horse's head I had no sugar on me.

It was winter. I was walking along a country lane. I often took this sort of walk, always to the same place. The earth is inexhaustible, just like the sky. There is always something new, something to hope for. A sheet of ice covered the ditches. From time to time I threw a stone at it. I enjoyed seeing the ice crack without breaking. The stones became encrusted in it like diamonds caught in a spider's web. That was how I was passing the time, my head bent over the stones and the ice and the sky reflected in it.

I had time and to spare: the insurance company I had spent twenty-three years working for had just dismissed me. I was too old to take on another job. No one had told me as much. I simply said it to myself: twenty-three years is a long stint. It's time you considered something else; surely you're not going to spend your whole life working, that wouldn't be serious.

Lobbing stones into ditches and catching what I called 'God's butterflies'– a well-turned sentence in a book, a smile on a face, a patch of sunlight on a wall – those things were a lot more serious, in tune with my mood at the time.

As for God's butterflies, all I had caught that day was a bad cold – oh, and this man with the horse's head.

He was down at the bottom of the field, walking, sunk in thought. I was reluctant to disturb him and was about to go on my way when the sound of my footsteps on the frozen ground caught his ear. He came up at a trot to the wooden gate, some two feet high. He was wearing black jeans and a white shirt. His mane rippled handsomely down his neck when he bent his head. His eyes were large and dark, like two plums off a tree. Friendship grows from tiny things. I took a liking to the man with the horse's head on discovering the mauve night in his quiet eyes.

I'm pleased to see you, I said to the lone individual in his field. I was about to say the same to you, he replied, tossing his mane in the wind. And we laughed together over our budding friendship. Or, to be precise, I laughed and he whinnied. It was already quite late. I had nothing but tobacco in my pockets. I told him I'd come back the next day with some sugar lumps. He smiled. As you please. You know where to find me: I never leave this field. As for the sugar, don't bother: I don't care for it. I only like apples.

Next day he was there, the same, bar a few details. He had changed his shirt and jeans. It rained in the night, he said to me. I don't like wearing wet clothes.

That day, and on the ones that followed, we kept the gate between us. One needs a degree of distance – a bit of air, a bit of absence, a bit of space or a wooden gate two feet high – for something to happen.

'Well, no job yet?' – that was the question my new friend put to me each time we met. 'Not yet, better still: never again' – such was my reply. With that we took up the conversation where we had broken it off the day before. Two subjects came up regularly: poetry and the circus. Two paths to intimacy with the stars, said the man with the horse's head to me.

Before I settled in this field, I worked in a circus. I did a tightrope-walking act with a friend, a woman with a mare's head. Each evening we took a little walk along a cable twenty feet above the ground. My friend started at one end of the wire and I at the other. We were to meet in the middle, exchange a kiss and return to our perches, this time walking on our hands. Ten years without a fall. Then something happened. Something insignificant to begin with. My friend complained that her back hurt her. She thought of consulting a doctor, but it all went too fast. Two swellings appeared which grew into wings in the space of a night. The public appreciated what they thought was an added refinement to the show. The children in particular were over the moon. Where they're concerned, nothing is impossible. The body of a young woman, a mare's head, two blue wings between the shoulders, nothing surprises them. There was a hole in the big top: the day before, a thunderstorm had battered the canvas and hailstones had torn it. A thin wind came through the hole. Nothing to bother about, the show had not been cancelled. We began our act. When each of us had negotiated our half of the wire, we embraced as usual – perhaps just a little more closely than usual – then my love beat her wings and in a second she had flown out through the hole in the canvas. The applause went on for a whole hour. I never saw her again.

At this point in the conversation my friend with the horse's head looked over my left shoulder as though something fascinating was suddenly taking place in the sky. I turned round. There was nothing. He took the opportunity to go off briefly to the bottom of the field. When he came back to the gate I could see an ocean in each of his eyes. I pretended not to notice anything.

After my love had flown away I couldn't manage to balance on the wire. In losing her I had lost my buoyancy. You see, it was child's play walking twenty feet above the ground when joining her was the object. For the joy of being close to her I'd have performed any feat. I did make several attempts to walk on the wire again, only to fall at the third step. The circus director suggested I transform the act by changing my costume. Dress as a clown, he said. Your falls will stop being blunders and be seen as gags. He wasn't wrong. Indeed he was absolutely right: true artists get their strength from whatever crushes them. They turn an obstacle to living into a grace. I tried. My falls were too real. I left the ring covered in bruises and made nobody laugh. I had to leave the circus and find other employment.

I've tried just about every job on offer for a man of my kind. The most enjoyable by far was as a cleaner in a small school. The children climbed on my shoulders during break and round and round the yard we went, galloping.

Fatigue came and with it an intangible withdrawal. I entered this field and now I never leave it. At first I read. Day and night. That passed. I don't want to be unfairly hard on books. I owe them some very good hours. We mustn't forget they come from trees. They remember this from time to time: there are books with sentences that rustle like acacia leaves. But I'm looking for so much more. Don't ask me what I'm looking for. I wouldn't be able to tell you. The only thing I know is that all the written wisdom in the world can't do anything for me: I am looking for something greater than can be written down. But I see the sky is clouding over. You should head for home. The apples you brought me today were delicious. Do you buy them in the market?

Time went by. My friend's mane began to turn white and I to feel the teeth of the north wind. We varied our talk about books with the odd exchange on the best remedy for rheumatism. There we were in agreement: there is no best. The body is like a boat. In childhood it is light, a floating dream, a sailing boat made of white paper. With the passing of time the paper grows soggy and the boat goes under. Live on good terms with your rheumatism, was the advice of the man with the horse's head: it proves you're a part of the living world. Nothing must get in the way of our talking and searching through talk. Nothing must spoil the pleasure of our being together.

I believe it was a Tuesday. I had never seen him so radiant.
I've found it, he said. I've found what I was looking for
– at least, not exactly, but I've found a word for it. You'll
never guess. I tried just the same: God? Death? Love?
No, no, he replied. You're looking in the direction of the
biggest. An unavoidable mistake, I suppose. I was making
it myself until this morning. It's so much simpler: I'm
waiting for spring.

I must have looked stupid. He became more specific.
His words came in a rush. I set them down here as
accurately as I can. Despite appearances there was no
madness present. I know that much. I have seen mad
people. They may be calm or angry, talkative or taciturn.
They all have in common a black, settled sadness. The
words I heard that day were full of life and gaiety.

What I call spring, he said, isn't a matter of climate
or seasons. Of course I'm not unmoved by the May
resurrection, by that new freshness in the air which
turns the heart so red and the girls into such teases.
But one can always object that this resurrection will be
soon followed by a new winter, an intravenous drip of
cold death. The seasons go round, stuttering. What I call
spring breaks that particular circle, like all the others. It
can irrupt at the darkest time of the year. Indeed it is one
of its characteristics to arrive unlooked for – to burst in,
break off and, ultimately, deliver.

I had brought a basket of apples for my friend with the
horse's head. Not Golden Delicious, too insipid. Little

russet ones, irregular, running with juice. He crunched
one before continuing.

I can see your astonishment. You don't understand me.
Let me reassure you: spring isn't something one can
understand: that's why it can be found in next to nothing
– a sound, a silence, a laugh. By the way, on the subject
of laughter, there was a little girl in the school where
I worked who had lost her mother in a conflagration.
I liked to watch her face at playtime. Her eyes were a
shade solemn but bright with laughter. She had only had
four years with her mother, yet it was obvious that those
four years had been more glutted with love than four
centuries. Looking into the face of this child, I thought
to myself: her mother, while she lived, poured a glass of
champagne into her child's soul – that's the sparkle in
the little girl's eyes. This thought that came to me then
was a spring-like thought. There is no conclusion to be
drawn from it. Spring doesn't give a fig about concluding.
It only opens, it brings nothing to term. It's of its nature
to be without finality.

But spring, as I call it, lacerates as well. It is at once sweet
and brutal. This combination shouldn't surprise us. If it
does, it is because life is distracting us and making us
inattentive. If we looked carefully, calmly, we would take
fright at the sovereignty of the merest daisy. There it
is, a foolish, yellow thing. To get there it has traversed
deaths and deserts. To get there, tiny as it is, it must wage
ruthless war. What I call spring is of the same order, a
thing that gleams like a daisy or a wrestler covered in
sweat. Nothing cosy, no certainty of outcome.

He chomped another two apples, the last in the basket.

Another sign of spring, what I call spring, is that when it comes we can't locate ourselves in it: we become – what's the word for them? – displaced people. Imagine a guest who, without warning, or giving you time to choose one for him, settles himself in your favourite chair. We all have our own favourite chair. Your immediate reaction is a slight displeasure. And then, very quickly, a sense of freshness supervenes. Almost nothing has changed, yet this almost-nothing changes everything. You take a different chair to your usual one and there you are, in front of a different landscape; yes, you are still at home, but in the best possible way – in transit. We get used too quickly to what we have. Thank God, spring comes from time to time to turn it all upside down again; we discover that nothing has ever belonged to us and this discovery is the most joyful event I know.

He fell silent and laid back his ears as though put out by something. I asked him if he was still feeling those twinges between the shoulders he had complained of yesterday. Not a bit, he said, that's gone. It must have been a chill.

I'd like to refine what I said on the subject of books: while they don't fulfil my expectation they do soothe and strengthen it. Read this: I copied it out for you last night. When I lit on this poem it took my breath away. Beauty has always worked on me like that. Actually, that's the way I see myself dying: something, one day, will come to meet me. This thing will be so pure that

I shall no longer know what to think of it or what to say, and it will take my breath away, for good. Don't worry: I have lived from the start with the sense that my death was round the corner and it's a happy feeling. It simplifies and frees. But just read the poem. It's by an English writer called William Blake. He lived in the Age of Enlightenment. He was a primitive. His poem doesn't speak of spring, yet nothing could be closer to it:

> *And no smile that ever was smil'd,*
> *But only one smile alone*
>
> *That betwixt the cradle and grave*
> *It only once smil'd can be,*
> *But when it once is smil'd,*
> *There's an end to all misery.*

I took the poem from the hands of my friend and began to read. You need two or three hours to read a novel. It takes a lifetime to read a poem. I was far from understanding this one perfectly, but one can receive a thing in its entirety without grasping it in every detail. In the time I spent reading the poem, it seemed to me that many clouds passed across the sky, numbers of stars appeared and vanished, days passed and nights passed. When I raised my eyes from the page my friend was gone. I called to him, I looked for him everywhere, but in vain. The field was empty. I sensed that our conversations had come to an end and I would never see him again.

I went to the market and bought an apple. I spent an age choosing it. It was a little russet apple, bruised and full of sweetness. I ate it slowly. It was my way of saying goodbye to my friend. 'Goodbye' is a word that life, that good nursemaid, teaches us to take our time in chewing.

Of the man with the horse's head I had but few keepsakes. An English poem and a few tufts of coarse hair caught on the gate. His words and their subdued gaiety stayed with me too. I went back home to note them down. Going home was not without its problems: for some time now my house had been floating a foot above the ground. It turned with the wind and the view through my window was never the same.

But that is another story for another day.

8

PURE PRESENCE

Except in his novels, the 'I' that is Christian Bobin is present throughout his work in one guise or another, if only as the acknowledged source of what is being said. In *Pure Presence* this 'I' appears as himself, there being no appropriate camouflage for visiting a care home (an expression Bobin naturally objects to). He is drawn there by his father, a loved and tutelary presence in both life and death, and never more so than when suffering from Alzheimer's disease. Bobin brings to this sadly common experience a rare sensitivity and an uncommon eye, as well as the gifts to translate it to the page in words as simple as light.

Alternating with the slideshow of the care home is a conversation Bobin holds with the tree outside his window, reminiscent of a much briefer exchange with a resident tree by Robert Frost. Trees are important to Bobin as paradigms of acceptance, which is not the same as resignation. Buffeted by the wind, stripped by the first frosts, they bear no malice; they are creation's givers, accepting their part in its everlasting renewal. The residents of the care home too are buffeted and stripped, but far from being diminished, they are invested with a new and mysterious dignity in a meditation on dementia both moving and profound.

PURE PRESENCE

The tree is outside the sitting room window. Each morning I ask it: 'What's new today?' The reply, from hundreds of leaves, comes back without a pause: 'Everything.'

It is at night, when the lamp-light thrown on the sitting room window prevents my seeing it, that I want to talk to it most. I know it is there, keeping watch in the dark, and the knowledge soothes me – like the effect on a deeply sleeping child of parental voices in the next room.

Yellow tints creep up its leaves like red up a shy cheek.

The leaves that are dancing, tipsy, in the wind's arms wouldn't change places with anything in the world.

Partly stripped of its foliage, it continues to breathe and sometimes even flies, borne by the angels for whom nothing is without secret movement.

My father, three months since, entered a home he will never leave. He has Alzheimer's disease. My father and this tree lead my thoughts in the same direction. From the one, shipwrecked in mind, and the other, surprised by autumn, I expect and receive the same thing.

Before he went to the home where he is today, my father spent several weeks among the dead, at Sevrey Psychiatric Hospital, near Chalon-sur-Saône, in the villa 'Edelweiss'. The dead were not the sick but the nurses who left them all day long without a caring word. The dead were these people in rude health and the flush of youth, who replied to my questions by pleading lack of time and staff and ended up saying crossly: 'In any case you can't understand. You're an outsider and you have to be on the job to have a proper grasp of the situation, the sort that counts.' The dead were these people entombed in their own professional deafness. No one had taught them that caring involved reading faces, talking – recognising in looks and words the undiminished sovereignty of those who have lost everything. My father, far gone as he then was, by pointing his finger at the one and only tree in the inner courtyard of the villa – a twisted shape of wood and suffering – had already given them their answer: 'you just have to look at that tree to see that nothing can live here.'

God blows past the sitting room window in a gust of laughter, disguised as a small yellow leaf, twirling.

First the trunk, then the main boughs, feeling their way through the space devolved to each, then the secondary branches, which spring from the first, but diverge on some particular to put out another viewpoint, and finally the highest branches which scrape the skin of heaven: all these gropings, strivings, failings – the working out of a thousand ways of getting to the light.

It's not just a tree outside a window. It is a counsellor I ask advice of and who teaches me through its own manner of proceeding, by way of hesitations and breakings off, towards the All Pure.

What is wounded in us seeks refuge among the tiniest things on earth and finds it.

Shortly before six in the evening I accompany my father to the dining room of the house of last resort. Most of the patients have already been assembled, some for half an hour. They sit facing each other, four or six to a table. Their eyes are blank. They don't converse. Some droop forward over their empty plates, like broken-necked dolls. The word 'hell' hangs in the air of this room. It is a very precise word, the only one that can utter this place, this moment and these people. There are two things as needful to us as are water and light to trees: solitude and interaction. In hell both are absent. My father sometimes jibs on the threshold of the dining room. He refuses to take another step as though seized with a foreboding that nothing will ever cut him free from this dead community – save his own death. His fit of temper subsides when he catches sight of the faces of his table mates, always the same. He has been in their company all day and presses their hands insistently each evening before taking his seat as though he had just found them again after a long absence. They respond to his handshake with a weak smile: even in hell, life can resurface for an instant from some hidden source, intact. A gesture suffices.

The Eighth Day

The calamity of believing one knows anything at all.

The tree looks rested.

Snow came and covered it in the night, like a mother drawing a blanket over the body of her sleeping child.

It presented itself to my eyes this morning in dazzling guise: like an angel newly arrived on earth and vainly hiding its hands behind its back so as not to betray its noble origins.

Our eyes and the world come to birth simultaneously, in an experience of utter newness, when seeing and seen give birth to one another.

The tree knew every one of its leaves by heart. It had a name for each. The wind has tossed them down on the cold earth. The snow has smothered them. The tree is still thinking of them. It is listening in its core to the resonance of their names.

I stand at the window with those who are gone. We are all leaning over the sill for a better view of the tree. When I stand up again, I am alone.

The wind and the tree have had words in the night. A branch was torn off during one of the stormier exchanges.

Seated for hours in the corridor of the house of last resort, they wait for death and dinner time.

Their life hovers round them like a bird above a felled tree, looking in vain for what had been its nest.

Shreds of fears, of small desires and proper names – they are at the mercy of their own speech as of everything else, and their answers wander wide of the questions put to them.

They like to touch hands held out to them, to hold them lingeringly in their own and press them. That language doesn't let them down.

Lassitude and approaching death make kings of them, kings without courtiers.

The wind relieves the tree of some of its snow, like a hand dusting down a party outfit.

She figured in the haze of my childhood: a friend of my parents, she kept a shop in the neighbourhood. In my memory she had a certain air. I rediscover her, shrivelled in an armchair, the facial bones standing out under her drawn cheeks. In the house of last resort the 'grande dame' has made way for a little mummy. She recognises me. Stripped of words, she looks at me and starts to cry. Bending down to kiss her, I meet the 'grande dame': she is there, in the depths of the mummy's watering eyes, silently screaming.

I like to lay my hand on the trunk of a tree I happen to be passing, not to assure myself that the tree exists – I have no doubt of that – but that I do.

The white snow has disappeared and been replaced by its little sister, dirty snow. She is a sickly and deprived child. There is no light in her face and she attracts no looks as her elder did. Unloved, she fades away fast.

At the tips of the branches a gathering of raindrops chatter merrily before jumping into the void.

The little mummy has died. For two days and nights she lay sleeping in the mortuary; then she was laid in the earth and the 'grande dame' took her first steps in the invisible world, fresh and rested.

Contemplating the room where patients receive their families – vast and empty on that occasion – my father remarks as though in dream: 'I am looking at what doesn't exist for me.'

He no longer recognises himself in photos; nor his family either. When they are pointed out to him his eyes light up with joy; he is filled with wonderment at discovering he has children, as it were new-born.

What he knew of the world and himself has been erased from his mind by the illness, as a sponge wipes a blackboard. It is a big board, impossible to clean in one go, but many sentences have already vanished.

A branch has broken off the tree. It didn't slide to the ground straight away. Other branches held it up and kept watch over it for several hours.

This morning the wind is talking to it as a friend. Its branches barely move, just at the tips, like someone nodding assent to the obvious: yes, yes, yes.

They often recall their mothers. Their other ties have now unravelled. They are left with long-dead mothers whom they talk of in the present tense, artless as little children.

What is on view here is no different in kind from what is seen elsewhere. The hurt, the dulled voices, the iron will to survive, all this is as commonly met with outside, in shielded life. Only here there is no escape: nothing but life wrung dry, spent clinging each to his own small rock until weariness talks the fingers loose … and then the engulfing in the great white wave of death.

The noxious thing gnawing away at their consciousness leaves enough behind for them to know, at fleeting moments, the horror of being where they are.

Death, the insider here, is never mentioned in their presence. They are the only ones to bring it up, always out of the blue and in low voices, as though it was something shameful.

These people wounded in soul and body possess a grandeur, which those who carry all before them will never attain to.

They communicate with their eyes, and what I read there teaches me more than books.

Today in the biggest of the lifts, the one used for coffins, there was a smell of formalin. I carried it home with me, where it blended with the scent of the lilies on the sitting-room table.

They call the house of last resort 'the care home'. The sick, the old and the dying who people its rooms are called 'residents'. The harder something is, the more banal the name we attach to it.

I get into the lift, press the button for the second floor and prepare myself for another meeting with the world turned wrong side out.

I visit every other day. My mother is with me. She carries a plastic bag in which she has slipped my father's 'tea-break', which she never forgets, together with the teaspoon used to pop it in his mouth, for he is so inattentive (that is to say engrossed in all that's going on) that he soon spots his clothes. In these moments my mother takes her place in the long line of women who, since time began, have been feeding life with its fare of light, well into the dark.

The stout lady with the ready smile who holds my face in her two hands. The little man whose Parkinson's shakes him like a tinkling bell. The grim-faced woman with hands crossed on the knob of a stick as stiff as she is. A man who buries his head in his arms like a child invaded by a feeling bigger than himself. Another who takes from his pocket things he has pilfered from nearby rooms and wishes to present to me. All, or rather each, need to be written about with discernment, slowly.

They may have lost much, with more to follow, yet the intrinsic character abides – a way of being, sometimes so intractable that release can only come through death, in the way a strong-jawed man cracks a nut between his teeth in one sharp movement.

The tree is an open book. Today's wind is leafing absent-mindedly through the pages as though its thoughts were elsewhere.

My first acquaintance with the house of last resort came through the smell clinging to the walls of its lifts – a clean substance used to mask a rancid: the sweat of death lingering under the well advertised deodorant of life.

The tree at the window is preparing spring. It is meditating in the winter cold on what it will soon be giving.

In a few weeks it will be offering to the world more light than all the books ever written. This light will pass and the following year the tree will give out another, again. This is the name of its work and the name of the work of the living while there remain to them a season, a day, an hour: giving, again.

Familiarity comes easily to the sun, whereas rain likes to keep a distance. Snow is on the shy side, even though it takes up all the space, something at which the shy excel.

A tree dazzled by snow, the awful innocence of a blue sky and the face of those whom death has started cosying up to: these have been my bedside books these past months.

Yesterday my father had a touch of 'flu. It increased his weakness. A wheelchair was needed to get him from his bedroom to the reception room downstairs. Then what is now his normal life took over: my mother's smile. Wafers and blackcurrant yoghurt. Scalding coffee served in plastic beakers. Talk with the other families present. That day my father spoke even less than usual. He was busy counting his waistcoat buttons. It seemed as though he would never tire of this occupation. He can barely read now. He has turned his back on reading as on so much else. All he could do that afternoon was count his waistcoat buttons, finger them to feel their thickness, slowly. There was nothing to the movement but a wealth of patience and fever. During that time, in the outside world, millions must have been pouring their energy into movements of every kind. None I am sure was performing a movement that radiated calm as this one did: the repeated counting of waistcoat buttons, like the absent-minded rolling of rosary beads between quiet fingers.

Sometimes it is a care assistant who accompanies him back to the refectory at the end of visiting time. He lets her take him by the hand, docile as a child in the presence of authority. Turning his back to me, he moves away with small steps, led by a strange woman towards an overcrowded and silent dining room. There is something tranquil and terrible about this picture, the last before the lift doors close, like a presage of approaching death.

'In all truth I tell you, when you were young you put on your own belt and walked where you liked; but when you grow old you will stretch out your hands, and somebody else will put a belt around you and take you where you would rather not go.' (John 21:18)

It is impossible to shield those one loves from unhappiness: I have been slow to learn so simple a truth. Learning is always a bitter business, paid for by us. I don't regret this bitterness.

I write in the hope of lighting on a few, just a few, only a few sentences clear and honest enough to gleam as brightly as a small leaf that the light has varnished and the wind scrubbed.

My father shares a bedroom with two others. A bedroom for three is not really a bedroom at all. It lacks enclosure, privacy – any sign marking the presence of one person, and no other. Three beds and three cupboards, each with a recess serving as bedside table. On my father's 'bedside table' are an alarm clock and a photo, which shows him smiling beside his wife. Yesterday he asked me who those people in the photo were, which grieved my mother and no doubt dismayed her. Anguish in her case is never far from impatience. A bit later, in the reception room downstairs, my father upset his beaker of hot coffee on the check tablecloth. My mother knew a brief moment of irritation, my father noticed her annoyance and was saddened by it. I was sitting opposite, watching them; I had my two parents facing me, two lost sparrows tumbling onto my heart, caught out by a brutal winter.

During the last months before he moved to the house of last resort, my father was often brought to tears by a memory he had never spoken of before. Sobbing, he would recall the fatal illness of one of his brothers. He himself was only five years old at the time. The illness was contagious. He had climbed on his brother's bed to hug him. A doctor had shooed him off with a smack, without explaining to the child why he had to keep his distance. Eighty years later this scene came back to overwhelm him. He talked of nothing else, unaware of how tired others were of hearing the same tale for the umpteenth time. For him each telling was the first, and each time his child's soul was pierced by the knife of injustice and bereavement.

Alzheimer's disease removes what education has implanted in a person and brings the heart to the surface.

Early in the afternoon blue launched its offensive. Within an hour it had swept across the sky and invaded the eyes of passers-by.

Winter sometimes fails to keep a grip, like a teacher during the last days of term.

I bring my father flowers and put them in a vase on his bedside table. I don't know if he looks at them after I have left. By then he has surely forgotten who gave them to him and accords them the same incredulous and weary gaze given to the rest of this room.

I have known the happiness of offering flowers to the living, the balm of placing them on a grave. The gesture of bringing flowers to the house of last resort belongs to neither of these orders of knowing.

In the lift, I ask him a question he doesn't understand. He frowns, gropes for an answer, fails to find one, comes up with: 'There's a grave inside me'. Then he falls silent. He has forgotten what he has just said. His eyes are on the lift door and the numbers lighting up above the buttons.

Now and then the enveloping mist parts and they come within touching distance of a truth so hard that they could hold it in their hands.

Of the four women seated in the corridor that day I kiss three, but merely shake the hand of the fourth, whose face, misshapen by illness, inspires me with a secret repulsion and puts me off touching it, even with a light brush of the lips. She senses this and quizzes me: 'Well, don't I get a kiss today?' I take her in my arms and kiss her, laughing in recognition of a beautifully taught lesson and the instant opening of paths between us.

My father, by contrast, has lost this concern for outward appearance. On a number of occasions I have seen him bending like an adolescent over patients with marked disfigurements and saying to them: 'You have a wonderful face, I'll never forget you.' This scene invariably upsets me to the point where I see, momentarily, the infirmity as being no longer in my father but in me.

The old lady who is talking very loudly in the corridor calls me by the name of her son, Basil. When I tell her I am not her son and that my name is Christian, she waves my objection aside, as though to say: 'Yes, I know, but that's beside the point: since I'm pleased to see you, you are my son; let's stick to what matters.'

Sparrows, squirrels and rooks: the tree is getting more mail with every passing day.

The tips of its branches reach down towards the road, as though it took pleasure in the talk of passers-by.

The first buds are springing: dense, tightly curled around a truth too delicate as yet to be uttered.

Out walking, my father likes to have his hand held, like children in the playground who pick their way nervously along a narrow beam, comforted by the weight of a loving hand in theirs.

It always takes me a few minutes to adjust my pace to his and join him in this dawdle proper to the beginning and the end of life.

I was born into a world starting to close its ears to any talk of death: it has had its way, not realising it had thus barred itself from hearing any talk of grace.

In today's world, where dreams are all of youth and beauty, death has to sneak in furtively, like an uncouth servant sent round to the back door.

I dreamed that God had Alzheimer's, that he no longer remembered the names and faces of his children, that he had forgotten their very existence.

An invisible hand has ripped the buds open, as one tears at a letter on which one's life depends. A flood of green light came pouring out.

The tree is conversing with the wind of things eternal and its young leaves tremble with pleasure.

Birds alight on it like footnotes in a scholarly book.

A number of religions claim that a few just persons are enough to save the world. It's possible that we have dropped below the critical number – unless we count this tree and its like among the just.

Yesterday afternoon, visiting my father, I was eighty-six years old. A little later, looking at a new-born baby, I had just turned two months. I am always the same age as those I am with.

Six or seven old people sitting in armchairs, facing the wall: I have learned to love this sight, always the same, that presents itself as the lift doors open. I rejoice at finding them again, shaking their hands and receiving their opaque communications.

Truth comes to us across so vast a distance that by the time it arrives it is drained and has next to nothing left to say to us. This next-to-nothing is a treasure.

I bring back from the house of last resort a need to touch the shoulder of those I meet, by stealth if need be, along with a deepened distrust of fine words.

If St Thomas placed his fingers in the wounds of the risen Christ, it was less to still his doubts than because there are moments when life has been so plundered and its presence is so searing that one can only fall silent – and touch with lightest finger-tips the glorious body of one's neighbour. They have their own way of knowing this, the Christs in armchairs facing a wall, in the house of ultimate resort.

Overheard from the tree: 'I don't understand everything the light says to me' – 'I never sleep: something or somebody is always turning up' – 'the wind has the eyes of a tearaway and the hands of an angel'.

Two years ago my father said he saw – saw positively, face to face – his long-dead parents.

He also declared, carefully underlining each word, that he felt 'outside time' and saw 'everything as new', even what was most familiar. The greatest mystics claim the same experience, word for word.

The name Alzheimer has the ring of a scientist at once mad and cruel.

The name Alzheimer allows doctors using it to think that they know what they are doing, even when they're doing nothing.

To get to you I push aside all the words for illness, age and occupation, as one pushes aside a curtain of strips of coloured plastic dangling in a doorway on a hot summer's day, until I find you in the freshness of the only word that doesn't lie: father.

Truth is what burns. Truth is less in words than in eyes, hands and silence. Truth is eyes and hands that are burning in silence.

Nightly, death seats itself at their bedsides. It watches them sleeping and having bad dreams. There are evenings when it murmurs a forename. That person gets up and follows without a word.

The trembling of the acacias in the garden of the house of last resort reminds my father of something – no doubt of the acacias that trembled near the place he lived in, only a year ago. The small green leaves shed in his mind a feeble light, seemingly from the depths of time: his years are much longer than ours.

The new-born and the very old are in a different world from us. In engaging with us they make us a priceless gift.

The sparrows invade the tree outside the window without robbing it of a peace in which their chatter plays a substantial part.

And when it is danger of growing too good to be true, the wind teases it as one ruffles the hair of a much-loved child.

The tree outside the window and the inmates of the house of last resort are examples of pure presence, having no defence at all against what happens to them day by day and night after night.

The acacia flowers, white and delicate, have the gleam of a child's kiss.

A few flowers, harvested by a nocturnal shower, lie fallen on a table in the garden of the house of last resort.

My father looks at them.

There is a light in his eyes that owes nothing to his illness and which it would take an angel to interpret.

9

RESURRECTION

The title of this piece should stop us dead. It is a failed attempt to translate the French 'ressusciter'. Between the two stands grammar, like the angel with the flaming sword. 'Ressusciter' is a verb and thus open-ended, alive with intrinsic energy, a signpost, pointing. It may in French be put to use with or without an object, giving it added freedom, whereas in English it lacks the intransitive option: you have to resuscitate someone or something. The noun 'resurrection' is stoutly fenced in theological space and, grammatically, is going nowhere: Bobin's instinct for the right word leads him unerringly to the one that is active, shape-shifting, and beyond translation.

The work dates from 2001, eight years after the publication of 'A World of Distance', years which have seen the death both of Bobin's father and of the woman he loved. The two texts invite comparison: in form they are not dissimilar, yet the mood is subtly changed – through the presence of death, it has become life-affirming. As though to emphasise this, the work is longer: more fleshed out in detail and thickly peopled, it is now a book's-worth. The presentation of apparent acquaintances, discreetly veiled behind initials, as examples of behaviour better avoided is among the moralist's traditional ploys. In this much-shortened version of the work the crowd has been radically thinned and nearly all those left have been met with in earlier pieces.

Central to the title's meaning is the reference to Easter. But word and concept come also with a sprawl of metaphorical outskirts and, in the original French, an ambivalence certainly willed by Bobin. Readers are to walk where they please: all vistas are inviting.

RESURRECTION

Easter mass: at the moment of communion those present rose in silence, walking down the side aisles to the back of the church, to return with precise, measured steps up the central aisle as far as the choir where they received the host from a bearded priest in steel-rimmed glasses assisted by two women, their features stiffened with the importance of their task – those ageless women who change the gladioli on the altar before they fade and give to God the care befitting an elderly, weary husband. From my seat at the back of the church, as I waited my turn to join the crocodile, I was looking at the people – their clothes, their backs, their necks, the profiles of their faces. Then, for a second, my eyes were opened and I saw all humanity at a stroke – innumerable individuals – caught in this slow, silent ooze: old and young, rich and poor, unfaithful wives and earnest little girls, madmen, murderers and eggheads, all scraping their soles on the cold, uneven flagstones of the church, like the unhastening dead emerging from their night to go and feast on light. I knew then what the resurrection would be like and the lightning strike of calm that would precede it. This vision only lasted for a second. Another second and my perception was back to normal, I was watching a religious liturgy so ancient that its meaning had been dulled and it only survived through a vague association with the first hectic flush of spring.

There is a star set in the sky for every one of us, at a distance where our mistakes can never tarnish it.

Going to the graveyard to visit a person one has loved is a strange experience. It starts as a gentle walk, nonchalant, almost dreamlike, until one is suddenly brought up short, faced by an insurmountable obstacle in the form of a tombstone. One was getting ready to meet someone and there's nobody there, indeed nothing at all, it's as though the earth was flat and one had absent-mindedly wandered to an edge. Standing in front of my father's grave is like looking at a wall at the end of a blind alley. All I can do is to throw my heart up and over, the way children throw a ball over a garden wall to have the faintly alarming pleasure of entering an unknown property to get it back. When I throw my heart over a gravestone higher than heaven, I have no idea what gravel it bounces on, I just know that it is not an empty gesture, for a few seconds later it returns to me, filled with joy and as fresh as the heart of a newly- hatched sparrow.

A day when we consent to do a small kindness is a day which death will never be able to tear off the calendar.

On the day of her mother's funeral, C. got stung by a bee. The courtyard of the family house was full of people. I saw the child, in the infinity of her four years, between the shock of the pain and the welling up of tears, scan the crowd urgently for her one sure source of comfort and then cut short the search, having learnt at a stroke the meaning of absence and death. This scene, which only lasted a few seconds, was the most poignant I have seen. There comes a moment for all of us when a knowledge past consoling enters our soul and rends it. It is in the light of that moment, whether it has already come to us or not, that we should speak to one another, love each other and if possible laugh together.

Over the course of a year I visited my father in the home where his memory shrank day by day, as vapour on glass shrinks at the sun's touch. He didn't always know me, and it didn't matter. I was well aware he was my father, and this allowed him to forget it. The connection between two persons may lie so deep that it lives on even when one of them can no longer see it.

My heart rarely wakes, but when it does it pounces instantly on the eternal as on a choice prey.

They boast of being free thinkers, and when one speaks to them of God, get as frenzied as a chained dog at the sight of a passing tramp.

I found myself once in a relationship where every word let fall by one of us was caught without fail by the other. The same was true of every silence. It was not the fusion experienced by lovers in their first fervour – an unreal and destructive state. In the spaciousness of this connection there was a kind of music, and we were at once together and apart, like the gossamer wings of a dragonfly. Having experienced this plenitude I know that love has nothing to do with the sentimentality that lingers in songs, nor does it come with sex, which the world has taken for its top promotion – the one that helps it sell all the rest. Love is the miracle that lets our very silences be heard, and us fine-tune our listening to the same degree: life in its essence, pure as the air that bears up the dragonflies' wings and rejoices in their dance.

My desk faces the birch tree and the birch tree faces God. I try to get my words in their alignment.

A bed of light, a chair of silence, a table made of the wood of hope, nothing else: such is the small room of which the soul is tenant.

The man people talk about when they discuss my books does not exist.

I have left myself in so many places, in the rooms in Dijon where, by way of studying, I sat up at night over captivating books, and along the country roads of Saint-Sernin, where I listened to G. laughing and talking, as I watched the feathered seeds of dandelions drifting over a pool. The self of those tranquil hours lives still where I left him. He is reading the same books in the same bedrooms and walks by the side of the same pool. I glimpse him now and then when the present grows transparent enough for me to see the farther side of time.

Seeing this world, one sees the other in transparency, like the watermark in the weave of the paper.

All I know of heaven comes from the astonishment I feel at the inexplicable goodness of some person or other, shown in a word or gesture of such purity that it is suddenly obvious to me that nothing in this world can have inspired it.

I write with a tiny pair of scales like those used by jewellers. Light I put in one pan and darkness in the other. One gram of light serves as counterweight to kilograms of darkness.

There is no greater unhappiness on earth than finding nobody to talk to, and our chatter, far from lightening the silence, in general only makes it heavier.

The black and white photo fits in the palm of a hand. Its edge is indented like certain biscuits. It was taken in 1954. I am thus three years old. I am wearing a romper suit and am bothered by the elastic that I am pulling at to stretch it. My left hand is holding my father's. He is dressed in a summer shirt and long shorts. We are on a country road, our eyes focused on the same distant spot, and our faces, a mixture of curiosity and concern, are not set to please. When I showed the photo to my mother, she exclaimed: 'At that age you were always with your father, you never left him.' My own thought, that I kept to myself, was that this was still the case and that it took far more than death to pull free those two hands wrapped so calmly round each other. There has been one obvious change: if we could take a photograph today, with a film sensitive enough to expose the invisible, it would show the same individuals holding hands, but having swapped statures: I am now the man of mature years my father was, while he is at the age death gives us, at whatever hour it comes, when it irradiates us with its innocence: two or three years old, barely more and maybe less.

There is nothing hidden, life is all there under our eyes, past, present and future, like three little girls exchanging secrets and giggling on a country road.

When we lose an object, a gold coin drops on the instant into the kitty of Dame Poverty.

The lime tree's buds have opened and the first leaves are emerging, small and crumpled, like the handkerchiefs that children pull from their pockets.

Little M., aged three, was walking with me round a museum patronised by Giacometti figures, poised confidently on the heights of their austere and friendly souls. Among them was the statue of 'the walking man'. As soon as she saw it, the child ran up to it as to a friend and, gripping the man's heels, she pressed her face against his legs, rocking the statue on its pedestal. Whatever gives children pleasure has to connect at once with mouth and hands. Beauty, which keeps us firmly at arm's length, is seen by them as beckoning and inviting. They don't gaze on the essential, they just grab it – the way they pick a daisy by its head, leaving the stalk standing.

The rain writes like a child sprawled on its page, in slanting uprights and with slow deliberation.

Resurrection

My father drank water more often than wine with his meals. This water came from the tap. My mother would pour it into a stoneware jug that she then set beside his plate. This sand-coloured jug held just enough for two glasses. It was so small in size that it could have served for playing at tea parties. Eighteen months after my father's death the little stoneware jug is still in the kitchen. It sits rarely on the waxed tablecloth now, spending most of its time by the sink, where it catches the light of passing days. When someone, somewhere, takes his leave – for a long-term job, say, or for death, the most absorbing of jobs – an object will bear witness to him in his absence, like the worn shoes in a painting by Van Gogh, shining softly on a farmhouse doorstep. I always get a faint twinge on looking at that jug, yesterday filled with water, today with shadow. I love these gentle taps at the heart's door. They don't open it to distress or melancholy, just to the mite of peace we feel at the touch of a cat's paw on our hand, when a tiny cushion of grey velvet sheathes the claws.

I broke off some holly in the forest and bore a few branches home, the way one carries in one's heart a spoken word, which stands out in its love, green and red, against all that one has heard during days bare of grace.

What wisdom lies in tales where one must keep from pushing the forbidden door or eating the over-glossy fruit: there are seemingly unimportant acts that must absolutely be avoided, at the risk of losing more than life.

Les Sables d'Olonne are by no means the most beautiful window open day and night on the ocean: money prowls, in the form of sums spent by tourists working at amusing themselves, and those amassed by estate agents, keen to stuff their pockets as full as their souls are empty. It scarcely matters. Winter habitually calmed all that, and, down on the beach, I was seized by the sound of the sea, as though someone dear to me had laid a sudden hand on my heart. The muted roar of the waves, by its indefinite repetition and the peace it stirred into the air, drew both on plainsong and on nursery rhyme. I was as moved, listening to it, as if I had heard the voices of those I had once loved and now are gone. Custom has it that the living should wash the dead before parting with their bodies. I have seen and heard, clearly seen and clearly heard, that through the ocean the dead were for ever approaching us with infinite gentleness, as though they felt the need to come and wash the living, and God knows the living need it.

Resurrection

It was their cheerful shouting that drew me to the sitting room window. There were four of them, aged thirteen or fourteen. They had tennis rackets and were laughing as they batted a dead rook between them, like a large ball of black chiffon. It lasted ten seconds or so, and then they grew tired of their game and went off, talking loudly and hooting with laughter, like executioners drunk on evil done. The rook was lying on the ground, its wings spread, as wretched as Christ after he had surrendered his spirit on the cross and far more abandoned. A passing shower gave it a mother's gentle care, caressing and washing its plumage. It lay a few yards from the lime tree, my ever-growing source of delight. It took me a while to focus on these two images together – that of the martyred bird with shining wings, like a banner thrown on the earth, and that of the tree, hallowed by light – without one image wiping out or veiling the other. Faced with life's worst cruelties, sometimes all thoughts come crashing down, as their framework gives way, and all we can do is ask the trees that tremble in the wind to teach us the compassion that the world doesn't know.

We do each other a lot of harm and then one day we die.

Between the village of Le Breuil and the town of Le Creusot there is nothing: one ends where the other starts. Sometimes, on Saturday afternoons, the children and I would spend hours cycling across this nothing. We'd pedal slowly along the main road, in single file like a row of ducks, and then speed off at random down lean and nearly empty streets which, being careless of any wish to please, had a charm all their own. The children raced each other round the square, long forgotten by the gentlemen in town halls who take decisions on renewal. Slightly out of breath from the ride, I would watch them from my bicycle propped against a decaying plane tree with a hollow trunk. The windows of the rundown houses round the square had net curtains that whispered now and then. The sky sailing overhead picked up in passing fine reflections of the area's nettles. God, who is someone with nothing to fall back on, must like this kind of place, that's for sure. He could take the air on summer evenings without risk of drawing attention to himself. After an hour or two I delivered the children back home. On the way we'd stop at a local café, patronised almost exclusively by cats and old men. Orange juice for the children, coffee for me, billiards for all was the standard order. When I returned home alone at the end of the day, I took with me a knowledge of heaven as deep as that of any theologian, as well as a grateful thought for the plane tree which, despite its own health problems, had kindly offered me a shoulder to lean on.

The wind visits every leaf of the plane tree without omitting one, like a pilgrim from the world's end who enters each house in a village to dispense his blessing.

In the old quarter of Geneva money is resting from its labours. A gentle stroll up and down these cobbled streets has its charm. There are moments, in the glade of a little square blessed by a tree in full leaf, where silence rises like a sun. Hard to believe one is in a village, let alone a capital city. We have left noise below, near the lake where a fountain is straining to spit in the sky's eye, where five-star hotel façades gleam discreetly and where bankers, like modern alchemists, work at conjuring gold from the blood of the poor to furnish settings for their watches, or hang round their mistresses' necks. Up above, in the old quarter, where the antique shops purr away, no echo of this tainted agitation can be heard. Money here is among its own kind. The dirty work has been done, it only remains to savour the fruit. There are people in plenty but not a single soul, and the faces of the passers-by come from the same tailor as their suits. This must be the world's heart, the coming true of the dream where it takes its pleasure of evil after banishing any unsightly misery that might cloud it. The Calvinist temple whose pillars rise like the words of a child-murdering father shut its doors at twelve sharp, just as L. and I attempted to enter. We had no regrets: we had seen enough and even the pastor's refusal was eloquent. Doubtless we should have discovered in this sacred space a God as closed to pity and love as this world is to real life.

Resurrection

I cleared a lot of useless stuff out of my life and God drew near to find out what was going on.

There was a couple living in the same house as my parents, on the floor above. In the rear courtyard shared by both families, the neighbour had planted a climbing rose against a wall. He drenched it regularly in a rain of insecticide. No bearer of grudges, the rose held out its blooms to each spring, tracing its script in yellow, orange and magenta lights across the greyish render of the wall. On summer evenings the two families got together in the courtyard and talked of this and that beneath the benevolence of the stars. Years passed without the little courtyard experiencing anything more dramatic than the unscheduled emergence of a rat from the cellar or a bird plummeting into the flowers of the hydrangea, to be picked out by my father, who helped it recover a taste for life by feeding it several times a day on breadcrumbs soaked in milk. Then, without our noticing, the world began to change. Age-old ways of thinking vanished over months, as might embroideries too delicate exposed to a light too harsh. Crafts, customs and beliefs: everything was fading as one looked. I was delighted, convinced that the world was undergoing a renewal, failing to understand at the time that the change was due to a mortal illness and that this vigour signalled its death throes: if there are still today, here and there, a few roses resistant to our errors, there are fewer and fewer of us able to read the scriptures in their petals.

Round Bissy-sur-Fley, some twenty kilometres from Le Creusot, there are unmade roads of yellowish earth along which little H. and I enjoyed going our light-hearted ways. The air was soft and scented and an orange light danced along the low walls edging the paths, like a young animal only too happy to follow us. We were no longer in wine-growing Burgundy, stony and tight-fisted, but in heathland unmoored from paradise and drifting slowly under a humid sun. The village of Bissy-sur-Fley was proud of its castle that had belonged to a poet friend of Ronsard named Pontus de Tyard. At that time H. was learning at school sickly-sweet poems by Maurice Carème or René Guy Cadou and the ruined castle attracted her as little as the language of the sixteenth century. Like me, she preferred to slip into the church where the floor, slightly cambered and laid with large flagstones that didn't meet, looked like the shell of an ancient tortoise. There was a rope in this church that we had fun tugging on: after a moment or two's hesitation, the bell, woken from its sleep in grumpy mood, would set the sky trembling. We'd do a quick getaway, accompanied back to the car by Pontus de Tyard and his Pléiade friends, all in high good humour with this lark that gave them a break from their literary labours.

I don't know what to think of death. It appears to me strange – but not really more so than love or the sky in the eyes of babies. Death, love and those eyes burning with blue have a purity that belongs to legend. I look at them uncomprehending, as in the fearful night of tales one looks at the lighted windows of a house in the far forest, out there, miles away.

There are souls in whom God dwells without their being aware. Nothing betrays the supernatural presence save the utter naturalness it breathes into the words and actions of those it inhabits.

One summer when I was working in the Dijon hospitals, my job was driving a van which I loaded in turn with dead bodies, loaves of bread and soiled linen. Several times a day I had to make a circuit of the town to a set timetable. I had written in a notebook everything I'd been told on the first day and used these notes during the entire time I worked there. Habit was no help: nothing fixed itself in my memory and I needed to reread my notebook every morning. I've always been like that when I've had to venture into the world, whether for work or study or any other purpose: in search of a user's guide I've never really found. I've spent my life inventing ways of disguising my non-participation in a world whose business and whose pleasures I've failed equally to understand. From time to time I try to learn the foreign tongue they nearly all speak. Any success is short-lived. This feeling about the world goes back a long way: doubtless to early childhood. I must have refused to learn something that can only be learned at that age. I don't know whether it's a grace or a disability. I only know that it is impossible for me to live in a world I don't believe in.

Language is like a vital organ to us and I found it sad to hear an engineer, too busy to fetch his children from school or find time to play with them, use the pretext of 'a simple question of logistics' – it was like discovering he had a fatal illness.

Each of us is born with a solitary task to fulfil and those we meet on our way help or hinder us in its completion: alas for the one who is unable to distinguish between them.

Resurrection

Lovable seagulls of the old port at La Rochelle, you saved me from the tedium of gazing on stones that over-admiration has rendered soulless. My mind went blank that morning when the port presented itself at the window of my hotel room: too often photographed, these old stones had ceased to dazzle, the way a wild animal loses in captivity the lustre of its coat. All they could manage was a ghost appearance on the shiny surface of postcards, along with an inset of Richelieu, robed in red and looking like an out-of-season strawberry, glossy and tasteless. I was ready to leave when I saw and heard you on the quay, close to my car: you were squabbling over a few scattered grains on the cobbles. Your cries were like those of babies and piglets. Some of you, eyes ringed with the same black velvet as your beaks, appeared to be wearing carnival masks. L. and I stayed watching you for several minutes. You weren't afraid of us. You carried on your pursuit of food a mere yard away, treating us to your incredible squawking and the slightly arrogant ungainliness of your earthbound strut. I thought I would be leaving La Rochelle bearing the image of a citadel locked into History like a miniature ship in a bottle. I carried away your cries and your childlike trust in nurturing life. The car picked up speed, the town distanced itself in the rear mirror, becoming once more a name on a map, and I went on hearing in my heart the carnival of your being.

10

A KILLER WHITE AS SNOW

Like *Resurrection*, this is a full-length book without narrative structure: a format perfected here, where space defines, orders, and sets apart. Vignettes, aphorisms and reflections are gathered in loose groupings: to each new selection a fresh page. A single sentence may be given a page to itself; it then becomes a marker, space acting as a spotlight. Books of this kind, laid out with care, become a total experience where the visual and the intellectual each enhance the other.

There is an opening paragraph in italics where the poet, who is also a prophet, steps forward: this, he seems to say, is what the book is about. Joy will win through. It is not that the underlying drone has been silenced, the struggle with 'melancholy' goes on, but the writer is sure now that the piccolo will triumph. He turns frequently to nature, seeking, and finding, confirmation. Sometimes it's a buzzard that provides it, more often a dragonfly or a group of weeds. He spends more time now with saints than sinners, but it is tigers

that take the palm here: on the last page a young one
bounds over death.

A KILLER WHITE AS SNOW

The bluish distance in tramps' eyes is beginning to freeze. Money locks jaws. The world is a slab of plaster lifting off a wall: what's beneath is hard as iron. Soon nothing tender will be left but clouds, flowers and the occasional wolf mask – faces that the manicured hand of money hasn't yet cleaned up, still adorned with their God-given wildness. To get an idea today of what the soul is like, you must look through old pictures, those showing miners with white china eyes starting in their blackened flesh, or new-born babies lying stunned in cribs aflame with lace. Books are huts for souls, feeders for the birds of eternity, resistance points. I hold out a paper hand to beings unseen. I have the ability to see through the iron wall: we are on course for beautiful things, once hell is behind us. My mother told me I was born between two gusts of her laughter, which doubtless explains the grain of this sentence: we are heading through the worst towards what is flowering and delightful, granted to the secret of our souls.

A Killer White as Snow

Pit-pat, pit-pat, drip-drip-drip: I listen with delight to the raindrop sounds of the black cat winkling itself from its sleep overhead and running down the oak stairs in the hope that I will feed it. Pit-pat, pitter-patter: faster and faster down the stairs, turning into the musical cascade that falls from Chopin's myriad magnetic fingers.

The whip of a mercenary rain is driving the roses to Golgotha where a panoramic view of life opens out.

Under the tapping of the lute-maker's fingers the spruce board returns a sound of tiny feet, pink and bare, running across freshly-washed tiles: the perfect recital.

On the wood of the page a few crumbs of blue and an upturned glass of silence.

The grandfather clock, a double centenarian, takes part in our conversation. There are four of us round the table. Five, with the clock, which repeats everything. Dish follows dish, talk peters out, only the hands carry grimly on, gnawing away at time with their unremitting tick, tock: death is trying to get into the room. The name of the last workman to repair the clock is written in white chalk behind the face: Claude Bonouvrier, aged 24, set it going again on November 15th 1892. Next to his name is the certificate of his birth at Saint-Gengoux-le-National, in Burgundy. One of the witnesses was Amable Farradesche de la Vayssière, jurist. His son, according to a newspaper cutting pinned to this document, was a 'consummate vagrant'. I have spent whole days dreaming about this 'consummate vagrant'. I still do. These two words are the perfect antidote to clock death. For a jurist with a double-barrelled name to have begotten a 'consummate vagrant' is among the most entertaining proofs of the existence of a God uncompromised by the secret melancholy of all our plans. Glory, yes, glory to the son of Amable Farradesche de la Vayssière, who emerged a consummate vagrant from the cavity of an old clock, shaking off before my wide-eyed gaze the chalky dust of his shroud.

On Alexander III bridge in Paris a man is grilling chestnuts without letting them char; he hands them out in a paper cornet with a double gusset – one for the chestnuts, one for the peelings, and offers a finger-wipe for good measure. With his calm and his outmoded taste for perfection he dismantles single-handed the whole sinister economic system of the world.

There is a gold key in the back of Johann Sebastian Bach and I turn it several times a day.

Five Oxford choirboys are building an ethereal chapel inside the church at Anzy-le-duc. Their voices, in time to within a thousandth of a second and fine-honed as razors, fall on Charollaisian soil and open up the souls of those listening. As we applaud, the boys' eyes light up with a sudden scapegrace triumph: the wholly pagan joy of having got through a minefield with their skins intact. They have been chatting to God in his sanctum and have received a golden silence in reply. Now, fanned out on the parvis to forestall any possible escape, they hold out cardboard collecting boxes for their audience to slip some coins in – a seraphic foray.

Bach is the ultimate peasant: for ever tracing the same furrow in the same field, carrying the same sheaves of light to the stabled angels and laying a golden cantata on the table each Sunday.

Dejected gundogs trot across the field, bells tinkling. In the distance, death is whistling them.

There will always be a shower to play the harpsichord or a blackbird to compose a fugue.

The soaring, delicate windows of the monastery chapel at Semur-en-Brionnais look scissored out of the blue. A nun has left them open, allowing the outside air to engage in learned murmurings with its indoor counterpart. This motherly care for the wellbeing of the premises is a better witness to the eternal than the always too triumphal humility of a retreat. God is not an idea, just a pink and blue vapour on the pursed lips of tiny children, a care given to ordinary life – the deep heart's breathing hole. Leaving the chapel I pass through the pallid face of a young nun. At the outer door a washed-out rose points me to the right path: 'Carry straight on, and don't stop at death, just keep going – it's always straight on.'

The customers wait patiently on the pavement outside the baker's at Saint-Sernin. Swallows are skimming the rooftop. As soon as one customer emerges from the narrow shop another enters. The first, arms laden with loaves swaddled in brown paper, sets off gaily towards his death which is waiting a few years down the road, smitten with this man living his unseeing life and with the joyous smell of warm bread clinging to his clothes. Through a window set in the sky between two clouds, a narrow shaft of gold falls on this scene, glimpsed from the car in which I'm heading to Le Creusot. Soon after, where the road climbs more steeply, I see the white cloud crash into the pink of a flowering cherry. A witness to the accident, I couldn't do a thing – just rejoice.

Seeing me coming, the dragonfly stiffens on the gate. I stop to look at it. Eternity's cart with its wooden wheels passes soundlessly between us: then the dragonfly returns to its own affairs and I continue my walk with a new shade of blue in my soul.

I was washing up two china cups in my hand-basin at the retreat house when the chink of cup on saucer freed a note whose joy turned the washroom into the radiant heart of a Jansenist sun.

'Cold! Cold!' is the children's cry to a seeker moving away from hidden treasure. 'Burning! Burning!' cry the angels to the one who hears two glasses ringing in eternity's tidy dresser.

The ring of the porcelain has woken all the denizens of heaven. I would happily spend the rest of my days drying these two cups of white snow, but the eternal doesn't last. Leaving the washbasin I return to the bedroom secretly exhilarated, like someone who has unintentionally slipped through the rain curtain of his death.

My mother, well on the way to her centenary hallowing, tells me that in her young days she adored the poems of Lamartine. As her lips form the name 'Lamartine', her girlhood eyes brim over. On Sundays, aged around sixteen, she would accompany her father on his fishing trips to the pool at Montaubry. Off by the early morning train, back late in the afternoon, again by train. The day dragged on through more than one eternity. Held prisoner by angels, sitting at her father's side, she saw boys and girls on the farther bank having fun. Their peals of laughter pierced her through and through.

A battle of light is taking place in the sky above Le Creusot, just over the rue Edith-Cavell. The name of this nurse from the Great War is in some way soothing. The coming storm adds a brilliance to the grey of the houses. In my pocket is a copy of Pascal's *Pensées*, a book I often carry in case of lull, famine, or too long a war somewhere or another. Pulling it out, I read as I walk: 'We can only love that which, in us, is not ourselves.' I close the book again. A cat is crossing a haunted garden. The singular grace of a neglected garden makes a strong case for a gypsy God. I ring my mother. She is in hospital at Montceau-les-Mines. I saw her yesterday. Her face held depths unplumbed by any scripture. It resembled a stone fallen from heaven that has sunk into the pillow. I set off again, my spirit lifted by I don't know what: the Holland grey of the houses in the street, Pascal's confident voice – or simply the intoxication of sipping at a life whose every instant is without a template.

In a post office in Picardy the painter Matisse, waiting for a phone call, picks up an envelope and whiles away the time doodling with pen on paper. Suddenly he sees his mother's face surfacing from the white depths. Those footloose minutes give him the key to his portraits: to catch the soul in a drawing one must let go of all thought and give one's hand to the angel of now.

Matisse practises his art like a higher form of medicine. A pharmacist takes Mercurochrome to daub a child's grazed knee where clotting blood has collected grit and stars. Matisse, with generous splashes of green, yellow and blue, daubs the lacerated soul of the viewer after wiping it clean of melancholy's grit.

The locum standing in for Saint-Sernin's doctor tells me that he failed his first year examinations after spending his time reading the whole of Dostoevsky. Someone interested in the life of the soul is sure to give good care to the body. Pondering on the invisible, failing one's exams – all steps in the right direction.

A stretching cat is a book of wisdom opening slowly at the right page.

Why does the play of light and shadow on a cat's whiskers move me so? It's as though in the space of a second, while watching those bars of black and white silk, I had understood everything about life, when in fact there was nothing to understand, merely a need to marvel at the transparency of days under a weightless sky.

To know one is alive is to know all.

There is nothing left to seek in life beyond the 'yes' that ignites it for good.

I hung my mind on the coat-stand before going out and went for the perfect walk.

The monastery of Uchon is the size of a swallow's nest. Inside the nest two nuns, black-habited, in a circle of flaming icons.

When death taps on the wood of an icon, it evaporates like a drop of water on a white-hot sheet of metal.

The monastery walls are decorated with frescoes. An apostle dipped in gold offers me his book, but I wave it aside a trifle briskly, having for now found better: beyond the open refectory window, on a rock at the bottom of a field, a donkey dozes. The wooden sash frames the living icon. The scent of a tuft of grass soon tempts the donkey out of the frame, leaving only the rock and a sky stuffed with blue over a russet Morvan hill: another icon, another day, for other eyes than mine. The donkey on its rock is more beautiful than the apostle glazed in thin gold on the wall: the one is alive, the other merely painted. The donkey carries placidly on its back a tonnage of air, distant stars and the meaning of life.

Now and then I see a thing so beautiful that I rejoice in knowing that it isn't mine.

Three weeds, tall and scrawny, are chatting at the foot of the traffic lights on Wilson Avenue. They have grown there, and, so exciting has life at this crossing turned out, they aren't going to move another step. The new-born child, deep in its abyss, knows this kind of ecstasy. Their nonchalance brings down to earth an atmosphere that owes nothing to the town's myopic preoccupation with itself. Faced with the painted canvas of the huge factory, they burst out laughing. A vanguard of eternity gone missing in enemy territory.

I do not know the woman I am speaking with on the telephone. The voice is a soul's way of navigating on the great, luminous river of atoms. This one puzzles me until my interlocutor says to me: 'I am blind.' Then I understand my pleasure in listening to her: her voice is a sun rolling through the darkness. The blind woman was giving out light.

In writing I am performing a job no one has asked me to do – apart, of course, from a few weeds and my late father's infallibly luminous smile.

A Killer White as Snow

The oak tree at the window is stripped for the winter. I bend over my book. Raising my head again I discover the tree streaming with green: winter has lasted a second.

Some thirty years ago I was bathing in the dark waters of the pool of Montaubry, when a coypu suddenly emerged close by. He looked at me, provoked, with his boot-button eyes and his whiskers dripping with a fairy-tale ignorance. Whenever I think of that summer the coypu breaks the surface of time: its emerging head bathes in eternity.

The man in the room next to my mother's died two weeks after his arrival in the home. Enough time for me to see something of his elegance, his weariness and his soul, worn as thin as a used bar of soap that keeps slipping through the fingers. His name has disappeared from the door of his room, and the gleam of the newly white card sears like a mystery.

Under its down the robin found dead by the garage door retains the warmth of halcyon days. God is a killer white as snow.

'That's how it is, sir … that's how it is,' said my taxi-driver, a slight Chinese woman, using the phrase – picked out each time with crystalline laughter – to punctuate the tale of the ordeals she had endured in childhood. I have Montaigne's *Essays* in my bag. Montaigne is the lemon Pascal squeezes when writing his more acid thoughts. The Chinese woman's almond-blossom laugh rivals in wisdom both those thinkers. In a room in Strasbourg I have been living the mysticism of hotel existence: I learned that, deprived of our usual surroundings, we become nobodies. That is the insistent message of walls, sheets and the indifferent courtesy of hoteliers. Shipwrecked in a double bed, waking to the old rose biscuit of the cathedral seen through the window, I sampled a ghostly peace. From a distance, Strasbourg station, encased in its convex glass surround, looks like a liqueur-filled sweet. Close up it is harrowing, like railway stations everywhere.

On station platforms there are only orphans.

The old lady is always the first to arrive in the dining room of the retirement home. The water in the jugs, filled far too early by staff under pressure, is already lukewarm. In a corner of the room is a water cooler. Steadying herself with her right hand against the walls, the old lady labours to carry each jug to the cooler, where she empties and refills it. Then, out of breath, she goes to sit down, having furnished each table with fresh water. Bit by bit the other residents come in. The water pots on the tables are filled with light. It's what is close to us that saves us, not the great things we dream of. 'That's how it is, sir … that's how it is.'

Each day is a struggle with the angel of darkness, the one who slaps his freezing hands over our eyes to prevent us seeing the glory hidden in our wretchedness.

The prophetic blue of the new-born baby's eyes seeks out its mother's face brimming with fatigue.

Whenever I leave the retirement home I carry away a dozen or two dazed faces in my basket. Once on the page, with a little ink on their cheeks, they recover their natural colours.

They take you from your home never to return: the only solution from now on is to make 'home' the air you breathe and the sky your eyes bore into.

Roses are the intoxicating proofs of God's existence. Their fire, black-fringed, smoulders against the wall of the retirement home. My mother, another resident, my sister and I sit facing them under the midnight-green rain of the cherry tree, with a bottle of champagne placed on the gravel like the mad knight in a giant chess set. Gaiety takes possession of drinkers *before* they drink: it is in the courage that floods the skull, the lightning decision to confront the rising dark by holding up to life a mirror with four pairs of brilliant eyes, triumphant at having discovered between them the centre of the world – that straw target made of humdrum days in which eternity's arrow, striking deep, vibrates unceasingly. Chinking glasses, we checkmate death.

A Killer White as Snow

On the wall opposite, two lizards are playing at 'one, two, three, *sun*'. A blackbird, its wire claws hooked to a branch of the cherry tree, intones an Ave Maria. A russet wavelet of squirrel arrives, a bounding park-keeper looking round to verify that all is as it should be.

The eyes of the dormouse shine like a night at the opera.

All our life is spent in going home.

A single sigh from the cat and all the invisible knots in the air fall apart. This sigh lighter than thought is all that I look for in books.

Stepping through the door, I receive full in the face the rays of a vision forged in 1443. Thunderstruck, I stand looking at the little red and white beds that might come out of a tale with God as ogre, the beams swallowed by painted wooden monsters, the painfully human presence of a varnished chair beside each bed, ready for the grand scene of the death-agony. A minute is all it takes for the long hall of Beaune's Hôtel-Dieu to yield its essence: miracles take up no time at all, grace has hair flying across her face. The mistake of course was to return a few days later to the scene of the excitement as a latter-day pilgrim on a tamer and more leisured visit. Miracles don't like being checked on. Beaune town-centre resembles a fan of close-packed, desiccated sweets in a presentation box. You could break your teeth on it. The small towns that tourism catches in its resin die of perfection. In a room of the museum missed on the earlier visit a weasel-faced archangel is weighing in his scales the souls of the newly dead. A horse in a tapestry has a leg cleanly severed, the stump pissing blood. In other rooms waxwork nuns are on the prowl. Quick, quick, out through the door and back to the nurturing air.

Somewhere in the sky there is doubtless a cloud cemetery. How wonderful its tombs must be!

A very old lady enters the cutler's shop in Beaune. She has a head like a vine peach stone and eyes of grey fire. She is funny, distinguished, up for the adventure of a real conversation. She admits to being so lonely that she hears 'the noise of the light bulb' when eating in her kitchen. These words throw an infinitely keener beam on the draining inner lives of souls, than do great works of art hugging their niggardly light to themselves in the gloom of museums.

A certain distinguished artist in black-and-white is working in the Petit Palais. Dozing one day in the cloakroom, he hears through his sleep the swinging of a hanger from which a woman, very delicately so as not to waken him, has just taken her jacket: 'I was amazed by the subtlety of the movement *and thus of everything.*' Delicacy is the keystone of infinity. The universe with its exploding planets emits the sound of a gently swinging hanger.

God may be simply a matter of sensitivity, the finest of our nerve roots, a thread of gold a thousandth of a millimetre through. In some of us the thread is cut, in others the least thing sets it vibrating.

The duration of a life is that of a new-born baby's smile: at once brief and endless.

The woman you wait for on the station platform emerges in glory from the flow of passengers, like some benevolent visitant from another world appearing in our own. Children are reborn to their mothers in this way each time they come out of school: one face alone beating the drum, one star filling the whole sky.

Huge, solid, ashen-brown, the buzzard meditates on a gate. Wrenched from its stillness by the noise of the car, it takes flight. Brown rises off the waving wings like cocoa powder: of the bird nothing remains but this misty colour floating in air, a buzzard shape dreamt up by the void. Under my eyes a God with a passion for housework has shaken a little dark brown mat, which became at each jerk of his hand a buzzard with wings outstretched. A minute later I slow down to let a young stag cross the road with the supple movement of a gymnast. It too is cocoa-coloured like the buzzard. God is a child who multiplies semblances, only to tire of them at once – it is left to us to see through them to the fairyland source of pure reality.

The stout woman in a strawberry dress has no sooner entered the café than she is energetically shaking hands all round, conjuring up a brotherhood-of-the-last-days. That done, she props herself on the counter and orders a glass of red wine with the easy familiarity of working people and saints yet unrevealed.

I am drinking white wine with a friend. The balloon-glass glistens, misted over with a glacial light even more refreshing than the wine. God has set me in the desert: it is up to him to slake my thirst. The gesture of the strawberry-coloured saint reminds me that nothing fundamental separates us humans. We are one and all the shipwrecked of eternity and the simplest gesture – so long as it is true – is a bit of heavenly flotsam to grab hold of.

Since we know nothing, ever, we may as well trust and be like God, blind.

The sulphur in the fine Mâcon starts up a faint drumming in my temples while an unknown woman's golden handshake blazes its way through my soul. There is nothing simpler than approaching a stranger with extended hand, yet the gesture is so rare. I once witnessed a sudden declaration of friendship in a psychiatric hospital near Besançon. A man walked up to

me, joy exploding in his face: 'I know you, you are God.'
My negative reply plunged him in gloom. Today I'd say:
'It's true, I am God – just like you.'

Cafés at night, seen from the street, are like the works
of minor Dutch masters – a modicum of gold set in lead.
One scene recurs again and again: a sad king drinking a
sour wine in a drear light.

Behind the shimmer of appearances the void, and behind
the void a palace of light, home to fools and saints.

What's left of all the books once read? Ash on the mind,
blown away by a puff of wind.

I have often taken delightful walks with Teresa of Avila;
she would speak to me of her life, her convents, the
angels who chivvied her. I have watched her deal with
daily business. She went about it with no half measures.
The strawberry saint in shaking my hand took me as
far in a second as the somewhat austere doyenne of the
mystical heights.

I flattened a mosquito on the wall with a book by Teresa
of Avila. There's no escaping the saints.

The angel's fingernails are black from the effort of digging us out of the rubble of our projects.

A Killer White as Snow

I was once a hare in paradise.

It happened on a dry autumn day on the fringe of the Pays Basque, where that landscape first takes shape with its icing-sugar houses, the theatrical walls of its pelota courts that confront the sky and its churches where the men present arms to a madonna painted in pink and blue. I go into one of these churches: I have barely glanced at the varnished wooden gallery where the men's choir assembles each Sunday, when I hear the scrape of their feet and the deep-sea roar of their voices. I watch these fire-eaters casting their manhood at the feet of the plaster Virgin facing them. The silence is still trembling with their homicidal choruses.

On the way back there is an old mill. To see it properly you have to cross a meadow before getting to a moss-grown wall blackened by green water. It is picturesque, calm, pleasing – but nothing special: that lies under my feet, in the tall grasses thick with mint whose overpowering scent makes my head swim. In that second I know what a hare, driven by its habitual eye-popping panic, would experience on scampering without stopping through this scented jungle: only on emerging would it realise it had been in a hare's paradise.

The year 1600 saw the shoemaker Jacob Boehme looking at a pewter vase on which a sunbeam lay broken: the vase, while remaining in the here and now, found itself suddenly on a shelf in paradise. It lasted the space of an instant. This instant made a seer of Boehme, who spent the rest of his days writing about this mad God who initiates our subtlest raptures.

A blackbird runs under the dark wood of the rosebush. The yellow of its beak sets my heart on fire. It is one of those prophets that dictionaries of mysticism overlook.

Yesterday, thanks to a quick movement, I caught a bit of Christ's tunic. It was a patch of silence.

The absolute shattered on the tiled floor with a sound of expensive porcelain. In any case, it was never used.

My heart and a stone seemed two of a kind on the day the circling hawk caught my eye. Each orbit it described in the blue brought me back to life. Its silence was so pure that I heard nothing else. The god gliding in the sky in search of prey withdrew slowly, after feeding me with its view, on wings more fluid than a silk flag in the wind. I watched it disappear behind the wood, my heart rinsed by the wildness of it.

On the bank of the pool of Saint-Sernin a man, sitting cross-legged under his umbrella, is threading a worm on the hook of his fishing-line. He is so bound up in his action that his death will never manage to find him.

In the hallway of the retirement home, a bewildered lady laughs at my greeting. Delusion and loss are close kin. In a room on the first floor a van Gogh poster – sunflowers in a brass pot – wrestles in vain with a woman in an armchair, her head lolling on her chest like an unstrung puppet's: the sunflowers' potency bows before the little broken soul. Further off, four or five to a table, residents sit waiting for the dinner trolley. Each face bears a weight of thought greater than the entire Vatican library. We have turned the last step to heaven into a stair to the scaffold. These women lack a painter by appointment of the sort that serves royalty, who would heighten in gold the souls that have now fled to the depths of their eyes.

A Killer White as Snow

None has chosen to be with the others. To be unable to change our destiny sets us alongside Christ with his pierced hands.

A saint is no freer than a bee.

Some twenty saints-by-necessity are sitting waiting for the 'white ladies' – their name for the female employees – who are going to bring their hot soup. Spring is coming in through the window like an open-handed thief. The sky hands out royal gratuities to its distant subjects. I don't need to go to the end of the world. I am already there and all is shown to be immense.

I leave the retirement home with my basket and its thermos in which dregs of bergamot tea are dancing around. A startled lizard jumps down a drain – another one that mustn't be forgotten. In passing I catch against a rose in a clump. Petals fall, the sky is losing its roof-tiles.

Perched on a branch of the cherry tree, the blackbird is brimming with song. The tempestuous waters of paradise burst from its throat.

I want far more than the young with their sacred overreaching. I want there to be enough blue in my heart to allow the golden hawk to soar there every day.

A walk along the Loire near Marcigny. Pebbles like tiny skulls. Cormorants wheel in the sky, annoyed by the walkers. The light on the river moves with killer speed. Life is bleeding gold. Our death cannot be so powerful a thing since it halts neither spring's unfurling nor the shining nonchalance of the Loire.

There are six of us walking down the muddy path. Each carries in his breast the holy medal of a mania faithfully observed. I know some normal people; they are more frightening than anything.

My eyes grab a fistful of winter-bleached reeds on the river bank and I line my soul with them: the nest will never be beautiful enough.

On our return we drank coffee in front of a chimney-breast the height of a twelve-year-old child. What did we talk about that day? I can't remember now. I only know I laughed so much that I fell off my chair. We made as free with time as if we would never lack it. And after all, eternity is ensured us. We sense it, and it isn't the minor contradiction of death that will make us see things differently.

It is because each of us strives *at any cost* to suffer as little as possible that life is hellish.

A Killer White as Snow

Whenever anguish shows up I put it in a suitcase and slide it under my bed. From time to time I pull the suitcase out, put it on the bed and open it. There is either nothing in it, or a luminous little fruit tree.

The cherry blossom and the hail that shreds it are saying the same thing.

No one could ever put my father's face underground. It rose into the sky like a sun.

I recognise at a glance the people seated along the corridor leading to the scanner: these are the grey figures from the station platform at Auschwitz. Hospitals take us so far from home that our souls struggle to keep up.

The leaves are falling from the oak and the jay's nest appears. Growing old is an illumination.

When the Japanese painter Hokusai died in 1849 he had, through his drawings, made life ten thousand times more vital than it had been before him. That, no doubt, is the work that each of us should spend a lifetime doing: rubbing the gold piece put in our hand at birth, so that it shines ten thousand times more brightly when death comes to steal it.

Hokusai paints fish and fishermen, flowers and birds, courtesans and artisans, octopuses and devils, lots of devils, sometimes dressed as priests. Then comes his last work, 'Old tiger bounding in the snow'. He is eighty-nine years old when he catches it with the tip of his brush. The tiger is as lithe as an angel might be, as though bones, flesh and soul were no more than silk, fluff, breeze. It is leaping between two low branches of a tree covered in snow; the spiny tips, piercing the white, look like claws. Everything has turned into tiger, everything has turned to snow. The lightness of the great cat – it slides through the snowflakes without touching a single one – is that of the hunter converted by the sight of the prey and delivered in that moment from its killer instinct. Hokusai, at the end of his life, believes life is made only of beginnings. 'When I am ninety I shall have penetrated the mystery of things; at a hundred, I shall certainly have a divine understanding of them, while at a hundred and ten, every dot and stroke I paint will be alive.' As I write this, Hokusai, continuing to paint long after death has rinsed his brushes, is two hundred and fifty years old. The old tiger grows ever lither; its spring is the arc of a rainbow.

In the corridor of the retirement home I pass a room with the door open. A sense of defeat hangs in the air. Like an angel half stunned by blows and pushed back on the ropes, a tired old man is making for the window. His back is to the television, where the sound is turned down, leaving only the picture. A white tiger walks slowly across the screen. This vision blinds me and the blinding renders me clairvoyant: no war is ever lost for good. One night the white tiger will re-enter the old man's room and he will be saved by its coming.

Graves are opening one by one like flowers.

The soul is a young tiger bounding over death.

11

THE JOY-MAN

L'Homme-joie, 'The Joy-Man', waves his banner over a collection of pieces or chapters – seventeen, of which eight follow here – disparate in subject but centred on the theme of joy. Joy has never been absent from Bobin's work – what could be more joyful than the paean to spring in 'The Eighth Day of the Week'? – but its voice has picked up strength as volume has succeeded slim volume. Now it is personified. The joy-man appears in person in the first chapter: 'You and I have a Sun-King seated on his red throne in the great chamber of our heart. And now and then, for a few seconds, this king, this joy-man, descends from his throne and takes a few steps in the street. It's as simple as that.' A Sun-King, a Roi-Soleil? Louis XIV springs to mind but is a false trail, a glint of authorial irony. Bobin is drawing here on Christian sources, the Sun of Righteousness or Justice [Malachi 4:2], taken up in the fifth of the great Advent antiphons, *O Oriens*, and the passages of St John's Gospel on joy [15:11; 16:24; 17:13] and on God's indwelling in the human heart [17:21–23]. The joy-man is surely the Risen Christ, taking a stroll in the street in the opening pages of the book, laughing at the philosopher out of the blue depths of the sky at the close – 'it's as simple as that'.

The numinous has been from the outset a significant presence in Bobin's work. By staying long undefined it provided a zone accessible to readers of varying beliefs or none, and no doubt the ambivalence was also Bobin's own. That this position has shifted over time is reflected in the titles, subjects and contents of later publications. He began by extending to the religious sphere his penchant for the marginalised, the non-conforming, starting with a piece on Marguerite Porete [in the collection *La Part manquante*]. There followed St Francis of Assisi, a radical in his day [*Le Très-bas*], and the community of Port-Royal, brutally suppressed in 1710 by a combination of King and Pope [*Les Ruines du ciel*]. Other titles, *Ressusciter* and *Le Christ aux coquelicots*, speak for themselves.

In 'The Joy-Man' there is a section – two brief pages entitled 'Better than an angel' – on the life of Christ. It comes to its point quite quickly with the words from the Cross, 'My God, my God, why have you forsaken me?' Bobin's theology is summed up in the metaphor that serves as commentary: 'These words are the heart of love, its flame that trembles, flattens, and does not go out.' The metaphor has a far wider embrace than one individual's belief; it taps into Gospel and doctrinal truth, evoking a Christ hanging on the Cross between life and death, praying in faith to his Father for a why, yet dying without an answer. The answer is the heart of love, the flame 'that … does not go out'. Yet, for all this, Bobin eludes capture, and rightly so. He is not a confessional writer. He is a poet, and, as poet, speaks not to a coterie but to all who find in him an echo of their questioning selves, a writer anxious to engage in dialogue and capable of catching a skylark on the wing in a net of words, yet delicately, carefully, ensuring that he 'does it no harm'.

Writing is like drawing a door on a wall too high to climb, then opening it.

The Joy-Man

Let's start with this blue, if you will. The blue of a freshened April morning. It had the softness of velvet and the brilliance of a tear. I should like to write you a letter composed only of this blue. It would be like the twice-folded paper used for wrapping the diamonds in the jewellers' quarter in Antwerp or Rotterdam, paper white as a wedding shift, with grains of angel salt in it, a Hop-o'-My-Thumb fortune, diamonds like a new-born infant's tears.

Our thoughts rise like smoke. They cloud the sky. Today I have done nothing and thought nothing. The sky came and ate from my hand. Now evening is here, but I don't want to let this day slip by without giving you the best of it. You see the world. You see it as I do. Nothing but a battlefield. Black knights everywhere. A clashing of swords in the depths of our souls. Well, it's of no importance at all. I walked past a pond. It was covered in duckweed – now that was important. We massacre life's delights wholesale and they come back more abundant than before. There is nothing enigmatic about war – but the bird I saw fly off this morning through the underwood, flitting between the serried tree trunks, left me dazzled. What I am trying to tell you is so tiny that I am afraid of hurting it with words. There are butterflies whose wings break like glass at the least touch. The bird flitted through the trees like a manservant slipping through the columns of a palace. It made no sound. It was costumed in gold as simply as a poem. There, I am getting close to what I wanted to say to you, to the next-to-nothing that I saw today and which has opened all death's doors: there is a life that never ends. It can't be caught. It flees ahead of us like the bird between the pillars in our heart. We rarely measure up to life. This doesn't bother it. It never ceases for a second lavishing its gifts upon the murderers we are.

The pool blossomed beneath the sky and the sky preened itself before the pool. The bird with prophetic wings set fire to the forest. For a few seconds I managed to be alive. I am aware that you may find this letter crazy. It isn't. It's more a matter of our wants being crazy. All I want here is to speak of what we call 'a fine day', 'a blue sky'. These expressions point to a mystery. A knife of light whose cool blade opens up our hearts. We lie buried under thousands of stars. And sometimes we notice and turn our heads, oh, just for a few seconds. That's what we call 'fine weather'.

I imagine someone entering paradise all unaware. He has worries, plans. He's very busy. The clang of metal and the clink of swords attend him. War is so banal. Then suddenly a light like snow falls on a pool, and a bird with wings of gold shatters the world's walls. It is something unhoped for. A few seconds, surely, are all we need to live eternally. 'We know by feeling and experience that we are eternal': this reflection of Spinoza's is as gentle as a child asleep in the back of a car. You and I have a Sun-King seated on his red throne in the great chamber of our heart. And now and then, for a few seconds, this king, this joy-man, descends from his throne and takes a few steps in the street. It's as simple as that.

I only like books with pages soaked in blue – the blue that has stood the test of death. If my sentences smile, it is because they come out of the dark. I have passed my life struggling with persuasive melancholy. My smile costs me a fortune. The blue of the sky – imagine that a gold coin fell out of your pocket and that by writing it I gave it back to you. This blue enthroned would spell the definitive end of despair and bring tears to all eyes. Do you see?

Writing
by hand I count the
sheep I haven't got.

Soulages

If there's a nasty passage after death it must be the entrance to the Museum of Montpellier. Invited for a reading, picked up at the station, taken to a hotel room where the high dark panelling appears to have been carved with a knife like those Swiss clocks which shoot out a manic cuckoo every hour, I am left with three hours to burn before the meeting. Coming across a notice about the Museum and its collection of paintings by Soulages, I leave the hotel again and walk off under the blue. The Museum has an unpretentious muzzle, harmonious, composed, of the Bach partita kind. One step inside and I see that I'm done for, assailed by the black and white angles painted on the floor. The vast hall is empty and cavernous, like a looted tomb. It wouldn't surprise me to be asked to leave my soul in the cloakroom. I am given directions to follow, and listen so attentively that nothing penetrates. I wander off at random. And there they are. Up in the sky, on the top floor, the paintings of Soulages.

What we see changes us. What we see reveals us, baptises us, gives us our true name. I am a child in a laundry, faced with black sheets hung on a line to dry. The pictures are great living animals, recumbent, a bit dazed at being there. A golden light falls on their flanks. Their breath comes heavily, slowly, drenched in silence. I stand before them at a loss as they cud on the black grass of eternity. Montpellier has disappeared, more thoroughly engulfed by the fabulous peace of these canvases than by a flood.

A massive peace descends, as in front of a gold Calvary. The vision of Soulages is stronger than death, halting it, as in time past one halted a vampire with a cross. This black constructs my brain, it lays its girders there, their mourning a mere semblance: the black is the flash of a ceremonial sword, a decapitation that opens the ball of lights. These works call on the open air, their cliffs shout for a gale. This isn't the work of a contemporary I'm looking at, but of the most primeval of painters. His paintings are Zen houses, or rather three-quarters of a Zen house to be completed by the spectator. An attendant, black-complexioned and -suited, is pacing the room, hands behind his back, a martyr to unclocked time. The two of us are surrounded by these divine and prehistoric beasts whose tarmacked pelts sweat light.

I am drawn, irresistibly, towards this other human being. I ask him what he thinks of the paintings. 'We are not permitted to offer our opinion, sir.' On my insisting, the poor man stutters out: 'We're human beings, we have thoughts and feelings too, even if we're not allowed to say what we think about the paintings in this museum.' I leave him, not to torment him further. I pass before a final painting whose black, oily streaks give a view of the lowered security blind of God's shop-window. That evening a woman tells me that her son has loved Soulages since he was three years old and that she doesn't know why. Soulages was not much older when he painted a snow-covered landscape all in black. I understand the child in front of me, I understand the child that Soulages was, and I can give no explanation. Explaining throws no light, ever. Real light comes only through illuminations, interior explosions, non-determinable.

Night, death and museum attendants have the same way of approaching us and telling us it's nearly closing time. I set out again for the hotel. Montpellier's plane trees hoist the bowl of my skull up to a Milky Way fizzing with white stars, magical with incandescent sparks, white on a background irrefutably black. I re-enter my Swiss clock and fall asleep thinking, as every evening, that the best is still to come.

When they
see a miracle, most people
shut their eyes.

Vita Nova

I've read more books than an alcoholic's tally of bottles. I can't do without them for more than a day. Their adagios have something of the healer about them. I have spent summers in their cool chapels, hollowed out of the chalk cliff-face of silence. Now from the dresser where they are taking on the patina of an icon I pull out the works of the poet who repainted the apartments of heaven and hell. Opening at random *The New Life*, I release two children and dust them down before I let them run into the light.

Dante goes down into hell the way one goes to the cellar to fetch a good bottle. I accompany him, and as we cross a space of burning tombs I hear shouts from the bottom of the garden. The first time, I think I am imagining it. At the second, I go to the window and realise it is hunters calling back loose dogs. I know these dogs. One of them nosed round one Sunday in front of my house. Short-coated, down in the mouth, as dejected as a captive devil on a Romanesque capital, it set tinkling a collar hung with what looked like petrified tears. I had given it a piece of brioche. This offering left it overwhelmed, used as it seemed to be – knowing no other paradise – to the ill treatment of its master. Its eyes bleached of hope, it was a mere killing machine deserving of compassion. It was clambering back out of Dante's hell, up the cleft of one of his songs. The hunters had stopped calling. They must have found their dogs and piled them back into their automotive cages. Beside a river of fire Dante discovers these people who have spent their lives doing neither good nor evil. Those 'who lived only for themselves', whom heaven rejects and hell spews out, their destined punishment being to flee naked from pursuing clouds of wasps and hornets. I shut the book and return to a world filled with the bustling of the same poor devils that I found in the poem.

Driving back from Autun. On my lips the name of the one I drove to and fro along this road twenty years ago. The trees that remember her laughter rain down patches of warm colours on her shade. A school springs out of a bend in the road like a grief in ambush. A cemetery meditates among a herd of cows. The smell that rises from the earth following rain persuades one to live unworried for the next ten thousand years. I slow down at the sight of a sign saying: 'Hunting in progress'. A boar with bristles black as tarmac bolts into the road five yards ahead of me. Our lives cross. He risks his skin whereas I am thinking of the happy hours of reading that await me. God-in-a-panic crashes into the undergrowth. The gun-toting heathen have lost his trail. I no longer understand this life where, *at the same instant*, some hear the wasps of death buzzing round their temples, while others are savouring an endless prospect of delectable reading.

We walk through life with bloodied hands. The flood-tide of our death will wash them clean.

Souls
are compasses that tremble
at the moment of insertion.
Only the saints describe
the perfect circle with
them.

The Hand of Life

Two angels with balls have come down to earth to restore order: Menuhin and Oistrakh are playing a Bach concerto in an old black and white film. The two violinists play with such intensity that one would think they weren't playing at all, just taking in sound. Oistrakh listens to his violin more feverishly than a mother waits on the breathing of her new-born child. Heaven's employees in tails, these two lift the world as one picks an inconvenient stone off the path to lob it aside. Their white hands fly out of the crow's wings of their sleeves. Menuhin lowers his eyelids under the weight of a thought, and raises his aristocratic features towards the master of silence high up in the flies. I see the swan's beak of the hand, the bow brutally thrown off by the strings it is caressing: I know that Bach is mad, I can hear it – he is mad with anguish. His music hurls itself at God in the way a toddler takes off on new-found legs, counting that the fall will take place just in the crook of its mother's arms, in their encircling welcome. And pushed by the hands of fright, the child rushes towards the abyss, to be caught in the nick of time by the motherly arms of silence.

I have in my mind a photo of my father in the same black and white that makes gods of the two musicians. He is outside, in the snow. He is rubbing his hands together to warm them, or rather one hand is wrapping the other in its reassuring grasp. This gesture sets him alongside the two virtuosos, dead today as he is: the sight of them gives one warmth enough to cross the frozen wastes of the world. Night is as black as the reverse of a red rose. I hear the wick of the Magdalene's night-light sputtering in the painting by Georges de la Tour. I see the empty spaces between people, vaster than the distance that separates a star from its neighbour. Each is working, working, working to his or her dark advantage, and any that don't are crushed. Bach is a child whose anguish is so acute that he gets the eternal to come to his bedside.

At home an angel, fag in mouth, was doing the dishes. My father would hold three washed glasses in one hand and say to me each time: 'You must never squeeze, otherwise they'll break.' It's the same with writing. My hands find pleasure in picking up the flowered plates and resuscitating them in a rain of hot lemon-scented water. Washing up is a metaphysical activity that restores to a material object something of the brilliance of the first morning. In the distance a television is doing its dreary job, like an executioner impassively cutting off the divine heads of silence and dream. A stream of adverts rends the air, a shower of sorry miracles rains down on the earth, their prophets smooth young creatures flashing precisely measured smiles. We must be really miserable if these are our compensatory dreams. The leftovers slide into the bin while behind my back on the airwaves the sales dummies are laying their infernal table. Lack of truth in a voice is worse than the end of the world. One doesn't twist a sunbeam. The washing-up is born twice daily: a tidal pulsing of the inscrutable banality of days. I like to wash up in the old way: by hand. The dummies in gold masks promote amazing things. It is as though they had found a remedy for death – but death is not an illness. A crystal glass breaks in the sink, a little blood beads on my finger – a red cloud on a sky of flesh, a poem stuttered out by life. Animals, clouds and plates are familiar with life's collision course – witness how they mope, tear and chip. I am a partisan of cowpats, books made of paper and dishes washed by hand. I have never seen anything true apart from wounded life, reddened by mishandling.

One day a doctor, seeking to calm the pain of a kidney stone, made a mistake and gave me the wrong injection: instants later my face and chest were brick red and my blood pressure had dropped to thirty. To counter the allergic reaction the doctor broke an ampoule and my father held my hand. My eyes were shut and I had ceased to hear. All I felt was this fatherly hand. I made myself small enough for it to shelter me, body and soul, and took my refuge there. That hand, with its weight and wrinkles, had become my place of safety, my certainty, my creed. The hands of Oistrakh, the hands of Menuhin hold likewise the hand of life, prevent its passing from red to black to deathly chill. Beauty has the power to resurrect. Seeing and hearing is all it takes. It is distraction that keeps us from entering heaven while we live, only distraction.

Cherry blossom condemned to die laughs all the more merrily.

The Eighth Day

The Arrested Minutes

A reliable touchstone for true beauty is the measure of hatred it attracts. The face of christ, before being illuminated by agoraphobic monks, was lit by the white gold of spittle.

Snipped from the air's green paper with careful scissors, the acanthus leaves surge round the footings of Maguelone's cathedral. 'It grows like squitch,' says a woman, spitting with words on the beauty of the flowers. Greyish mauve with modest bonnets, their silent shouts celebrate the everlasting. Brambles, rust and rain have always formed an escort for the air god. The ordinary and the poor raise the dust of their nothingness to salute the stars, their kin. The best minutes of my life, the arrested minutes, were spent squatting on the leprous pavement of the rue d'Allevard in Le Creusot showing a baby girl the splendour of a dead leaf – time's rich calligraphy which fissures the fronts of houses and adds its footnotes to the bottom of stone pages.

Place an enormous rose-red leaf of Virginia creeper in the pudgy hand of an infant a few months old and watch its eyes roll with surprise and then with delight. See how the baby rends the flesh of this pink light and gleefully dispatches the miracle, and observe your own simplified heart filling with joy. Now that the leaf is shredded, returned to dust, the pink that belonged to it alone is released into the air: it is everywhere, on your lips, in your eyes, in your soul suddenly quickened. You have just assisted at the birth and death of the world in God's fat fingers.

I never think of God on entering a cathedral. I go in to feel the friendly old hand of the cold on my shoulder. Each time I look around for the dead who built it all and couldn't today lift so much as a snowflake. All I see is candles gathered in council: a little wax and lost gold, a child's treasure with a great tonnage of stone to keep it safe. I walk up the nave as though inside the head of a new-born infant where all is calm and wide awake. A baroque group is rehearsing the evening's concert. One of the musicians dons a horse-head mask to amuse his colleagues and blows a fairground air or two on his trumpet. On the marble wave of the altar a crucifix gleams as bright as the trumpet. The absent christ and the baroque joker improvise an ode to the marvelling death throes of each passing moment.

Maguelone cathedral, built of stones hauled up from the adjacent sea, is a great empty shell: God the Hermit Crab has left; there two minutes ago, he is off now down the garden. I always thought acanthus leaves, being an architectural term, grew only in Romanesque stone for the fanning of devils and saints. I come upon them in their natural state, giving the garden a jungle-like air. Peacocks stalk near the flowerbeds. Their cries have a funereal splendour. The cries of one torn living out of life. On a clear day one can see as far as God.

Silence,
that gift of angels we
no longer want and
don't try even to unwrap.

Better Than an Angel

One morning Christ walks out of the world's old, run-down house. He is about thirty years old. He takes nothing with him. It's the start of his hedgerow life, the shreds of which, after his vanishing, are gathered by his friends. The joy of the air as it brushed his temples, the whisperings of the water between his palms, the wonderment of the foxes that crossed his path – nothing of that has reached us. A scattering of sayings, most of which draw their beauty from the world of shepherds, fishermen and vinedressers are all that remains to us of the life on earth of the greatest of all poets. For to look life and death in the face and awaken the stars in the void of people's hearts is to be a poet. Comment has worn the wayfarer's sayings threadbare. They endure: the simple cannot be exhausted. Like hornets on a fallen pear, a bustle of theologians press round the tears on a face so human it became divine. 'My god, my god, why have you forsaken me?': those words of Christ are the most passionately loving ever spoken. Each of us feels their inward tremor. No life can afford to forgo this cry. These words are the heart of love, its flame that trembles, flattens, and does not go out. They are also the only proof of God's existence: one doesn't address non-being in those terms. One doesn't reproach the void.

197

After that, nothing – breath torn away, energy deserting what is now just rotting flesh. This final flare of speech makes of Christ something better than an angel: our anguished and vulnerable brother. 'My god, my god, why have you forsaken me?' This cry that shatters against the marble mouth of a mute God turns the one who hurls it into our intimate friend, the closest of the close: ourselves when confidence drains out of us like blood from an opened vein and we carry on talking as lovers to what is killing us.

The dark has to deepen for the first star to appear.

The dead are strange people. Their eyelids are as heavy as monastery stones. It's as though they were entranced by some book we can't decipher.

The Little Sweep

I have seen death dull two eyes the colour of mirabelles. They belonged to a little black cat, as skinny as a mendicant friar, which emerged from the woods surrounding the house I am writing in. Two years of enchantment followed his arrival, before death laid its hand on this jewel. In the last hour, when his body assumed the limpness of a rag doll, his eyes held their own until a lightning-strike, opening them wide, flooded the world with their liquid gold. His wonderment just then was that of a true thinker sensing that something is on the point of coming into being. Then his eyes swam in a black light that shone like lacquer. Through them a being resembling an Egyptian god looked out at me, unseeing – a judge of such profundity that he declined to judge. Kingdoms of the dark stared at me, indifferent. And that was it. That night a trust, a gentleness, an elegance vanished from the universe once and for all. When I look back to that evening a drawn-out flash passes through my brain and buries itself in the white conglomerations. I had suffered the privilege of seeing, in an instant, an innocence bled of its light. The great black wave set rolling out of the depths of time had taken back one of its own. The cat had rejoined the source of his beautiful eyes.

The Joy-Man

Life bears us off to death like a cat carrying her kittens by the scruff to a place of safety. From the butterfly's powdery wings to the care-worn foreheads of the dead, all things present us with the same enigma. The eyes of the little cat that were spirited away were bringing a revelation with no name to it. It is in the hope of finding this name that the purest poems get written, and when our hands reach for a book it is to touch the husk of the unpronounceable name. We have a slight advance on the great black wave we now and then hear growling in the distance. What should we do with this advance so quickly lost? What can we do that makes sense, apart from nothing: walk down a country lane, open a book, watch a rose burst its bodice? When he picked his way over the brown blanket of my bed the little cat left tiny pimples of light. With one prodigious leap he has leapt onto the knees of my absent father. I now know what a cat really is: someone who looks like a cat, who comes and steals your heart.

I raced
an ant across the terrace
and was beaten. So I
sat in the sun and
thought about the million-
dollar slaves of Wall Street.

A Bunch of Keys

I was reading a philosopher when the great wave of
laughter came sweeping through me. Silent, seismic,
subterranean. On reaching my face it produced no more
than a smile, a surface ripple, but underneath my heart
was burning, a furnace in my breast. The philosopher
was deserving of the highest esteem. He had found
a bunch of keys lost in the grass. Splendid keys, gold
ones, as big as the keys to a city and about as useless:
there weren't any doors. There never had been any. The
keys served no purpose – it was this that had set off the
great silent guffaw I was now sharing with the vase of
freesias on the window-sill. A bit of fluff came floating
past. To be a speck of dust can be a joyful thing. The
flowers were laughing in half-a-dozen colours. Outside
the window a spider was climbing up its silver rope. It
was heading straight for the sky like an incautious word.
It too was laughing at the uselessness of all philosophy,
as were the flowers and the Virginia creeper round the
window, and the blank pages lying yet uncooked on the
desk. Even the word 'desk' took on a playful, comic
note. I genuinely liked this philosopher. A peace at once
luminous, airy and beneficent inhabited his sentences.
But the great guffaw was stronger. It came from beyond
the stars, hurled like a stone. The books of philosophers
are like those cardboard masks held in place by an

elastic band. Behind the cardboard one gets short of air. Look, said the flowers, redecorating the room with their fragrance, there is no door, not anywhere. There are only our fragrance, our colours and our laughter. The other world starts with this laughter. The other world is this laughter. Why look elsewhere, for something else? The god is a child who is hiding and there comes a moment when he betrays himself: passing close to him one hears him giggling. You can hear him in music, in silence. In the bud that bursts, behind the cloud sailing by; in a gap-toothed mouth. Everywhere. The noise a bunch of flowers can make in a tiny room is unbelievable. Mine were going to my head. No philosophy under the sun can rival a single ox-eye daisy, a bramble, or a pebble conversing like a tonsured monk one-to-one with the sun and laughing, laughing, laughing.

I look at the sky's blue. There's no door there. Or if there is it has been open all along. From time to time I catch the sound of laughter in the blue, the same laughter as the flowers'. No one can hear it without joining in.

This blue, I'm slipping it into this book, for you.

I took the devil's hand.
Under his black nails
I saw a glint of light.

Translator's Notes

Translated works by Christian Bobin, in chronological order:

'The Eighth Day of the Week' [*Le Huitième jour de la semaine*], Éditions Lettres Vives, 1986; Gallimard, in *L'Enchantement simple*, 2001.

'Queen, King, Jack' [*Dame, roi, valet*], Éditions Brandes, 1987; Gallimard, in *La Présence pure*, 2008.

'Look at Me, Look at Me' [*Regarde-moi, regarde-moi*], Gallimard, in *Une petite robe de fête*, 1991.

'Get Moving, Jonah, I'm Waiting' [*Va Jonas, je t'attends*], Gallimard, in *Une petite robe de fête*,*1991.

'A World of Distance' [*L'Éloignement du monde*], Éditions Lettres Vives, 1993; Gallimard, in *L'Enchantement simple*, 2001.

'Mozart and the Rain' [*Mozart et la pluie*], Éditions Lettres Vives, 1997; Gallimard, in *La Présence pure*, 2008.

'The Tightrope Walker' [*l'Équilibriste*], Éditions Le Temps qu'il fait, 1998; Gallimard, in *La Présence pure*, 2008.

'Pure Presence' [*La Présence pure*], Éditions Le Temps qu'il fait, 1999; Gallimard, in *La Présence pure*, 2008.

'Resurrection' [*Ressusciter*], Gallimard, 2001.

'A Killer White as Snow' [*Un assassin blanc comme neige*], Gallimard, 2011.

The Eighth Day

'The Joy-Man' [*L'Homme-joie*], L'Iconoclaste, 2012.

The above texts have been translated in their entirety, with the exception of 'A World of Distance' and 'Mozart and the Rain', which have been shortened at the request of Éditions Lettres Vives, and the three last titles, shortened for reasons of length, whole books having no place in an anthology. Happily it has been possible to abbreviate these works, which are not narrative, or not continuously so, without any loss of integrity. The presence of asterisks in 'A World of Distance' and 'Mozart and the Rain' indicates a lacuna in the text. In 'Resurrection' and 'A Killer White as Snow', where Bobin groups his reflections, often giving a whole page to a line or two, I have respected his own page breaks and introduced others where cuts have been made, while trying to arrange the remaining passages sensitively. I would have been happy to hand this over to Bobin, but with a gracious wave of the pen he assured me that once a book was written it belonged to his readers and I should do as I liked.

Also quoted or referred to:

Christian Bobin, *Le Christ aux coquelicots*, Éditions Lettres Vives, 2002; Gallimard, in *La Présence pure*, 2008.

Denys Turner, *Julian of Norwich, Theologian*, Yale University Press, 2011, p. 22.

Stéphanie Tralongo, 'Des livres pour repenser le quotidien : le cas des réceptions de l'Œuvre de Christian Bobin', doctoral thesis for University of Lyon 2, 2001.

Reader review, on-line bookseller: www.amazon.fr/christianbobin/lagrandevie

* *Une petite robe de fête* – see above – has also been translated by Alison Anderson for Autumn Hill Press in the USA.